Illustrated Gloss

ARCHITECTURE

850–1830

Illustrated Glossary of
ARCHITECTURE
850-1830

John Harris & Jill Lever

FABER AND FABER
London · Boston

First published in 1966
by Faber and Faber Limited
*3 Queen Square London W.C.*1
First published in this edition 1969
Reprinted 1978
Printed in Great Britain by
Whitstable Litho Ltd.
All rights reserved

© John Harris and Jill Lever 1966

I S B N *(Faber Paperbacks)* 0 571 09074 5

I S B N *(hard bound edition)* 0 571 06883 9

TO
EILEEN AND JEREMY

ACKNOWLEDGEMENTS
(photographs)

Aerofilms and Aero Pictorial Limited   106, 112
Architectural Review   157
Hallam Ashley   156
William J. Barrett   158
B. T. Batsford   128, 131, 193, 210
British Railways   188
C. H. Cannings   87
Chandlers of Exeter   168
Country Life   49, 109, 130, 151, 173, 189, 190, 191, 196, 203, 204, 205
Courtauld Institute of Art   68, 76, 149, 207
F. H. Crossley   18, 27, 29, 44, 65, 70, 71, 74, 77, 84, 85, 91
Eric de Maré   102, 155, 178
Kerry Downes   138
Herbert Felton   2, 3, 4, 5, 6, 7, 14, 30, 35, 37, 40
Hants. Field Club   63
George Herbert   10
E. Shirley Jones   39, 66
A. F. Kersting   114, 135, 136, 163, 175, 183
Jeremy Lever   51, 101, 184, 212i, ii, iv, 224
Nathaniel Lloyd   53, 108, 142, 143, 215
National Buildings Record   8, 11, 12, 13, 15, 16, 19, 20, 22, 23, 24, 25, 26,
28, 31, 36, 38, 41, 42, 43, 45, 46, 47, 48, 54, 55, 56, 58, 59, 60, 61, 62, 64, 67,
69, 72, 73, 75, 78, 79, 81, 82, 83, 86, 88, 89, 90, 92, 93, 94, 95, 96, 97, 98, 100,
104, 107, 110, 111, 113, 115, 122, 124, 125, 126, 133, 137, 139, 140, 141, 144,
147, 148, 152, 154, 159, 160, 161, 162, 164, 165, 167, 169, 170, 171, 174, 176,
179, 180, 181, 185, 186, 192, 194, 195, 198, 199, 200, 201, 202, 206, 211, 212iii,
214, 217, 221, 222, 223
M. Parry   177
Alistair Rowan   153
Royal Commission on Historical Monuments (England)   17, 80, 129, 146,
187, 219
Walter Scott, Bradford   9
Seaman & Sons   134
Frank Smythe   99
Warburg Institute   57, 103, 105, 123, 145, 197, 208, 209
Reece Winstone   21, 32, 127, 132, 220
G. Bernard Wood   218
J. Yerbury   166

INTRODUCTION

THE idea of an architectural glossary finds its expression in 17th century France with the growing desire to classify information. Such was the success of the first comprehensive glossary of this type, A. C. Daviler's *Explication Des Termes D'Architecture* appended to his *Cours D'Architecture* of 1691, that was followed by editions in 1693, 1699, 1710 and 1720. In England the popularity of Daviler's first two editions must have prompted Richard Neve to compile his *City and Country Purchaser, And Builder's Dictionary* in 1703. Unlike Daviler, however, Neve not only presents a series of definitions, but discusses his subjects in treatise form. Following Neve, 'Explanations' became the fashion and we find one in John James's 1708 translation of Perrault's *Ordonnance Des Cinq Espèces De Colonnes* as well as in the many editions of Evelyn's rendering of Fréart's *Parallèle De L'Architecture* which had first appeared with an *explanation* in 1650. Following Edward Oakley in his 1730 *Magazine of Architecture, Perspective and Sculpture*, as much as Explanations and Dictionaries multiply, so does the art of glossarial cribbing. Salmon's *Builder's Dictionary* appeared with his *Palladio Londinensis* in 1734 and the same year saw the two volumes of the *Builder's Dictionary*, a large expansion of Neve's project, the first of the comprehensive English dictionaries and glossaries, and the forerunner of Nicholson and Gwilt in the early 19th century. The mysterious William Robinson (who may have been Edward Oakley) added an *Explanation of the Terms* to the second (1736) edition of his *Proportional Architecture*, and in that year Batty Langley's *Dictionarial Index* formed part of his *Ancient Masonry*. These books were at the height of the encyclopedic vogue. In 1756, however, Isaac Ware's *Explanation* in his *Complete Body of Architecture* could be regarded as the last presentation in an architectural treatise of this type of systematized information in the 18th century. The many later authors such as the prolific William Pain saw no need to elucidate their architectural vocabulary.

Because the Industrial Revolution occurred between Ware and Peter Nicholson, its new scientific outlook partly invalidated the earlier dictionaries and created a second spate of encyclopedias. Nicholson's *Architectural Dictionary* of 1810 is the first of the modern text books, and his new attitude towards scholarship and accuracy is epitomised by two further publications in the eighteen-twenties: Robert Stuart's *Dictionary of Architecture* (*c.* 1820) and Joseph Gwilt's *Principal Terms Employed in the Science of Architecture*

Introduction

appended to his 1825 edition of Chambers's *Treatise on Civil Architecture*, in which glossary can be discovered the germ of his great Encyclopedia of 1842. Between the two Gwilts, James Elmes's *Dictionary of the Fine Arts* appeared in 1826 and was followed in 1838 by John Britton's *Dictionary of the Architecture and Archaeology of the Middle Ages*, the latter a quintessence of the Battle of the Styles or the triumph of Gothic. In 1842 Gwilt uses for the first time the phrase *Glossary of Terms* when he published his *Encyclopedia of Architecture*, a book of such universal value that it ran through nine impressions and 1443 pages within the span of fifty years. Gwilt, as revised by Wyatt Papworth in 1867 and 1876, is still the main source for any architectural glossary, and is one to which we, the authors of the present *Illustrated Glossary*, are deeply indebted. Yet Gwilt's glossary possessed few illustrations, a deficiency recognized by John H. Parker whose *Concise Glossary of Terms* of 1846 is the first truly illustrated work. One can say that Parker established the standard form of architectural glossary, unaltered in essentials in any of the modern works such as Atkinson of 1906, or Ware and Beatty of 1944.

We were delighted, therefore, when Faber and Faber asked us if we would undertake the preparation of a new type of glossary which, by the use of photographs, would show an architectural detail not only *in situ* but also in relation to the whole façade or part. We felt, with our publishers, that modern glossaries were either appendages to a greater work or were text books illustrated with dull, pallid line drawings. We believe that the succinct definition of a term requires a standard of accuracy that few line drawings can maintain with consistency. We realised this would demand photographs of high quality and we hope we have achieved this within the limits of feasibility and cost.

The search for photographs began as an estimated year's job; it ended as a four-year marathon. It is incredible, and sometimes ludicrous, how as many as fifty photographers will stand in front of the same building, raise their cameras, and perpetuate an almost identical negative. Special commissions of illustrations were financially out of the question, so we sifted through nearly 200,000 photographs to find our details. Often we would be frustrated to find the illustration for definition, but perpetuated in a bad photograph. If a few poor ones have crept into our corpus we apologise and plead that in this thankless task we were often near the lunatic fringe.

We have tried to define and illustrate the terms of architecture in general use for the study of British architecture until about 1830. The definition of terms relating to the Modern Movement and of present day technocracy is a totally different proposition, and even in 1966 vocabularies are in such a state of flux that only an international body could hope to establish coherence. We have included few archaic terms because we feel they are not relevant for general reading in this century. If our glossary is criticised on this ground then our reply is for the critic to go and buy a secondhand copy of Gwilt or Parker. We have, however, included certain terms that are not yet acceptable to the compilers of the O.E.D. Our grounds for inclusion are that international writers such as Professor Pevsner or Sir John Summerson disseminate them and we believe in their value. Our glossary is not a pedantic one.

We have arranged our illustrations in a sectional way according to building units, forms or type. Because each section is, as far as possible, chronological, the evolution, for example, of medieval roof structures or interior decoration, may be assessed at a glance. We have sometimes omitted a term basically self-explanatory. We feel only a dullhead would want to see an illustration of a door or window. We do, however, point to the architrave of a window or the broken pediment of a door. If we have missed an occasional term, please forgive us.

We must obviously pay tribute to our predecessors in this task of glossary compiling. Quite frankly we have frequently disagreed upon the correct definition of a term. When this occurred we went through as many as fifty similar definitions until we felt we had compiled the right one. We were surprised to find that even the glossaries in current and standard use contained a percentage of contradictions and mis-phrasing of terms. Our task was not easier for that. Our warmest thanks go to the staff of the National Monuments Record, to their Director Mr. Cecil Farthing, to Miss Valerie Gillam, Miss Jill Pugsley, and to Mr. Nicholas Cooper. In sifting through their great collection of photographs they were extremely patient with our often outrageous demands and helped us with their usual courtesy and kindness. Mr. Lionel F. Bell has given us much assistance, and the clarity of our terms was improved by the useful comments made on the first draft of our manuscript by Mr. Hope Bagenal and Mr. Hugh Braun. Finally, and not the least, our thanks to our respective husband and wife, whose ears over the past four years have been deafened by our incessant pleas for advice and help. The most heroic contribution to this glossary was really made by Jeremy Lever, who, in his busy architectural career, agreed to the mundane task of drawing our lines and perfecting the technical layout of the illustrations.

ABACUS. The flat slab on top of a capital, on which the architrave rests. In the Greek Doric capital it is a thick, square slab; in the Greek Ionic and in the Roman Doric and Tuscan it is square, with the lower edge moulded; in the Corinthian and Roman Ionic it has concave sides and the angles are cut off. (117, 118, 119, 121, 122, 123)

ABUTMENT, BUTMENT. Any solid structure which resists the thrust of an arch or vault. (31, 147)

ACANTHUS. A form of ornament based on the broad scalloped leaf of the acanthus plant. Used on Composite and Corinthian capitals and as a decorative motif. (121)

ACROTERION. A simplified pedestal, with or without a figure or ornament, placed on the three angles of a pediment. The term may also be applied to the figure or ornament itself. (149)

AEDICULE, AEDICULA. An opening (door, window, niche, etc.) framed by columns and a pediment. (183)

AISLE. A division of space. The lateral division or divisions of a church, parallel to the nave and usually separated from it by piers or arcades. (1, 3, 4, 8, 9)

ALMSHOUSE. A house built and endowed for the poor and aged. (128)

ALTAR. The elevated table at which religious services are performed. (80, 93) *See also* Antependium, Predella, Reredos, Retable, Tabernacle

ALTAR-FRONTAL *see* ANTEPENDIUM

AMBULATORY. Literally a place for walking. Generally applied to aisle or walk around the east end of a church, behind the altar. (1, 6, 7)

AMPHIPROSTYLE *see* TEMPLE

ANCON *see* CONSOLE

ANGLE BUTTRESS *see* BUTTRESS

ANGLO-SAXON. The period from A.D. 449 to 1066. From the seventh century characterised by the use of rough fundamental forms, long and short work, pilaster strips or lesenes and baluster mullions. Because timber has perished, the style is represented only in churches. (15, 72)

ANGULAR CAPITAL. A form of Ionic capital having all four sides alike; the volutes being placed at an angle of 135°. This invention, attributed to Scamozzi, obviates the discrepancy between the front and side views of the antique capital. (195)

ANNULET. A small flat band, fillet or ring around a column or attached shaft. (70) *See also* Shaft ring

ANTAE. Pilasters placed at the ends of the short projecting walls of a portico. The base and capital of antae differ from those of accompanying columns. (148)

ANTEFIX. An upright ornamental motif placed above the eaves to decorate the ends of a roof ridge. Found in Greek and Neo-Greek architecture. (163)

ANTEPENDIUM. The covering which can be either an ornamental cloth or a painted or carved panel, on the front of an altar. Sometimes called altar-frontal. (80)

ANTHEMION. A favourite classical motif of alternating lotus and palmette connected by scrolls and forming a continuous pattern. The term, however, has now come to be used synonymously with palmette or honeysuckle to describe a single floral motif based on the palmette. (200) *See also* Palmette

ANTIS, IN *see* PORTICO

APOPHYGE. A slight concave sweep or extension at the top or bottom of a column shaft where it joins the capital or base. Also called congé. (117, 120, 121, 123)

APRON. A raised panel immediately below a window sill; sometimes shaped and decorated. (142)

APSE. Semicircular or polygonal termination of a church, usually of the chancel.

ARABESQUE. A type of surface decoration usually consisting of intertwined foliage scrolls, sometimes incorporating ornamental objects or figures. (200) *See also* Grotesque

ARAEOSTYLE *see* INTERCOLUMNIATION

ARCADE. A series of arches supported on piers or columns. (3, 159) Timber supports are called arcade posts.

ARCADING *see* BLIND ARCADE

ARCH. A curved structure formed of wedge-shaped blocks of brick or stone (voussoirs) held together by mutual pressure and supported only at the sides. SEMICIRCULAR ARCH: a semicircle having its centre on the springing line. (42, 51) STILTED ARCH: an arch sprung from a point above the imposts; the vertical masonry between the imposts and springing line resembling stilts. (44, 51) HORSESHOE ARCH: a stilted arch with the masonry between the springing line and imposts, inclined inwards. (51) ELLIPTICAL ARCH: a half-ellipse drawn from a centre on the springing line. (51) SEGMENTAL ARCH: the segment of a semicircle drawn from a centre below the springing line. (50, 51) TREFOIL ARCH: a rounded or pointed arch springing from the apex of two separated rounded arches. (43, 51) POINTED ARCH: composed of two arcs drawn from centres on the springing line. LANCET ARCH: a narrow pointed arch whose span is shorter than its radii. (51) EQUILATERAL ARCH: an arch whose span is equal to its radii. (46, 51) DROP ARCH: an arch whose span is greater than its radii. (51) THREE-CENTRED ARCH: two separated arcs with centres on springing line, surmounted by a segmental arch with centre below springing line. (48, 51) FOUR-CENTRED TUDOR ARCH: a depressed pointed arch composed of two pairs of arcs, the lower pair drawn from two centres on the springing line and the upper pair from centres below the springing line. (49, 51) OGEE ARCH: a pointed arch formed of two convex arcs above and two concave arcs below. (47, 51) SHOULDERED ARCH: having shoulders, i.e. with projecting stones resting on the horizontal course, sometimes called Caernarvon arch. (45)

ARCHED BRACE *see* ROOF

ARCHITRAVE. The lowest of the main divisions of an entablature. (116, 117, 118, 119, 120, 121, 122, 123) Also, the moulded frame surrounding a door or window. A SHOULDERED ARCHITRAVE is one in which the mouldings around a door or window turn away at the top at right angles, rise vertically and then return horizontally, forming a shoulder. (137, 170)

ARCHITRAVE BLOCK *see* PLINTH BLOCK

ARCHITRAVE-CORNICE. An entablature (116) from which the frieze has been elided. Favoured by Inigo Jones.

ARCHIVOLT. The under curve of an arch. (31, 68) Also, the moulded band applied to this curve. *See also* Intrados, Soffit

ARCH STONE *see* VOUSSOIR

ARCUATED. A term applicable to a building structurally dependent on the use of arches. *See also* Trabeated

ARRIS. The sharp edge formed by the meeting of two straight or curved surfaces, e.g. between the flutings of a Greek Doric column. (69)

ARROW LOOP, LOOPHOLE. A narrow vertical opening with deeply splayed inner jambs, in the walls or battlements of a castle, through which arrows were shot. (111) *See also* Loophole, loop window

ARTISAN MANNERISM *see* PROTECTORATE STYLE

ASHLAR. Squared hewn stone laid in regular courses with fine joints. (183)

ASHLARING. Upright timber framing used in attics to cut off the acute angle made by the junction of roof and floor.

ASHLAR PIECES *see* ROOF

ASTRAGAL. A small convex moulding, often decorated with a bead and reel There is a form of this moulding sometimes called a bagnette or baguette. (117, 118, 119, 121, 122, 123)

ASTYLAR. A façade without columns or pilasters. (134)

ATLANTES. Figures or half-figures of men, used in place of columns to support an entablature. Atlantes is the plural of Atlas. Also called Telamones or Persians. (198) *See also* Caryatid

ATTACHED COLUMN *see* ENGAGED COLUMN

ATTIC. A room situated within the roof of a building. Also, the upper storey above the main cornice. (134)

ATTIC BASE *see* BASE

ATTIC ORDER. An order of pilasters applied to an attic storey. (142)

AUMBRY. A recess in the wall of a church to contain the sacred vessels. (86)

AUREOLE *see* VESICA PISCIS

BAGNETTE, BAGUETTE *see* ASTRAGAL

BAILEY. The open area or yard of a castle, which when combined with a motte is known as a motte and bailey. In later and more complex castles, the space between the outer and inner walls is known as the outer bailey and between the inner walls and the keep as the inner bailey. Also called a ward. (106)

BALCONY. A platform projecting from an exterior or interior wall of a building, above ground level. Enclosed by a railing or balustrade and supported usually on brackets. (160)

BALDACHINO. A canopy over an altar or tomb, usually supported on columns. Known also as a ciborium. (105)

BALL FLOWER. An ornament of globular shape resembling a three-petalled flower, enclosing a small ball. Characteristic of Decorated architecture from around 1300. (89)

BALUSTER. A small pillar or column, supporting a rail or coping. (140, 182)

BALUSTER MULLION *see* MULLION

BALUSTRADE. A series of balusters supporting a rail or coping. (140, 147)

BANDED COLUMN. A form of rusticated column where the rustication is applied to the shaft in intermittent bands. (136, 172)

BANDED RUSTICATION *see* RUSTICATION

BARBICAN. An outer defence, sometimes in the form of a tower, to protect the entrance of a castle or tower. (106)

BARGE BOARDS. A corruption of verge boards. These boards are placed on the verge or incline of a gable to screen the projecting roof timbers, and to prevent the penetration of rain. Common in fifteenth- and sixteenth-century architecture, they are often beautifully pierced and carved. (218)

BAROQUE. A term principally applied to the style of architecture, painting and sculpture current in Italy, and primarily in Rome, in the seventeenth century. Its architecture is characterised by dynamic spatial effects, often achieved by the integration of painting and sculpture, and deliberately aimed at involving the spectator physically as well as emotionally. English Baroque is a later, shorter-lived and less well-defined style which is the creation of Nicholas Hawksmoor and Sir John Vanbrugh. It emerges around 1692 out of Sir Christopher Wren at Greenwich and the unexecuted designs for rebuilding Whitehall Palace. The third contributor was Thomas Archer who, unlike Hawksmoor and Vanbrugh, had experienced Roman Baroque at first hand. The style flourishes until about 1722 when it was clearly in the process of being superseded by Lord Burlington's Palladianism. Although it uses a different vocabulary, it shares with Italian Baroque a vital interest in the dramatic manipulation of mass, rhythm, space and silhouette in architectural composition. (138, 139)

BARREL VAULT *see* VAULT

BARTIZAN. A turret corbelled out from a wall or tower of a castle, church or house. (114)

BAR TRACERY *see* TRACERY

BASE. The lowest part of a structure. That part upon which the shaft rests in a column. The ATTIC BASE, applicable to all the orders except the Tuscan, consists of a scotia moulding between two tori. (118, 119, 120, 121) The TUSCAN BASE consists of a torus with a fillet above. (117) A third type of base often used on the Doric, Corinthian and Composite orders is composed of two astragals with a scotia and torus above and below. (116)

BASE COURT. An inferior court, usually at the rear of a house.

BASEMENT. The substructure or lowest storey of a building, which may be above or below ground level. (135)

BASILICA. In medieval architecture, a church with a nave higher than its aisles, and in early Christian architecture with an apse at one end. The name and form derived from the Roman assembly hall.

BAS-RELIEF. Sculpture in low relief, used in architectural decoration. (178, 195)

BASTION. A projection from the outer wall of a castle or fortification. (106)

BATTER. A wall with an inclined face. (162)

BATTLEMENT. An indented parapet, the openings are called embrasures or crenelles (hence crenellation) and the raised parts, merlons. A licence to crenellate was the equivalent of a permit to fortify a residence. (111)

BAY. An external or internal division of a building, marked, not by walls, but by units of vaulting, roof compartments, an order, windows, etc. (1)

BAY LEAF. The leaf of the bay tree, used as a decorative motif, often in festoons or applied to a torus moulding. (182)

BAY WINDOW. A fenestrated projection beginning on the ground floor of a building and sometimes embracing several storeys. (133) It may be square or canted, but when curved it is called a BOW WINDOW. (181) *See also* Oriel window

BEAD. A small convex moulding. (192, 196)

BEAD AND REEL. An alternating pattern of circular and elliptical motifs used on classical mouldings. (197)

BEAKHEAD. An ornamental motif of bird's head and beak, sometimes a beast's head and tongue, used as a moulding enrichment in Norman architecture. (42)

BEAM. A horizontal structural member, carrying a load. (180)

BED MOULD, BED MOULDING. A moulding or series of mouldings under a projection, such as the corona of a cornice. In the classical entablature, the mouldings between the corona and the frieze. (119)

BELFRY. The part of a tower or turret in which bells are hung. (16)

BELL CAPITAL. The core of a capital, which in the Corinthian and Composite orders is covered by carved acanthus. *See also* Drum

BELL-COTE. A turret expressly designed to hold bells, usually placed at the west end of a towerless church. The sanctus bell-cote is located at the east end, usually over the chancel arch. The bell is rung at the consecration of the Host. (98)

BELL TOWER *see* BELFRY, CAMPANILE

BELVEDERE. A turret or lantern on a house, to afford a view, or a pavilion on an eminence for a similar purpose. Sometimes called a standing or look-out tower. (126, 141) *See also* Gazebo

BENCH ENDS *see* PEW

BILLET. An ornament used in Norman architecture, consisting of short, cylindrical or rectangular blocks or billets, placed in hollow mouldings at regular intervals. (44)

BLADE *see* CRUCKS

BLIND ARCADE. A succession of arches, attached to and used to enliven a wall; a characteristic Romanesque decoration. Also called a wall arcade or arcading. (54, 67, 73)

BLIND TRACERY. An imitation of window tracery on a flat solid surface, e.g. on chancel screens, vaulting, wall surfaces, etc. Used in Gothic architecture. (33, 39)

BLOCK CAPITAL *see* CUSHION CAPITAL

BLOCKING COURSE. A course of bricks or masonry above a cornice. (138)

BOLECTION MOULDING. A convex moulding which projects beyond the surface it frames. Frequently used in seventeenth-century and early eighteenth-century joinery work. (192)

BOND *see* BRICKWORK

BOSS. An ornamental projection placed at the intersection of the ribs of a vault, or sometimes of beams in open wooden ceilings. (32, 36)

BOWTELL *see* ROLL MOULDING

BOW WINDOW *see* BAY WINDOW

BOX PEW. An enclosed seat with high sides, usually forming one of a series of box-like compartments in a church. (97)

BRACES *see* ROOF

BRACKET. A projection designed as a support. (182) *See also* Console, Modillion.

BRATTISHING. Ornamental cresting found on late Gothic screens, panelling, etc. Usually formed of leaves, Tudor flowers or miniature battlements. (81) *See also* Cresting, Tudor flower

BRESSUMMER, BREASTSUMMER. A massive beam spanning a wide opening and supporting a sometimes projecting superstructure. (169) *See also* Summer

BRICKWORK. A HEADER brick is laid so that the end appears on the wall face. A STRETCHER brick is laid so that the side only shows on the wall face. ENGLISH BOND consists of alternating courses of stretchers and headers. (212i) FLEMISH BOND consists of headers and stretchers laid alternately in the same course. (212ii) HEADING BOND is composed entirely of headers and was used during the eighteenth century. (212iv) GAUGED BRICKWORK is brickwork built accurately and laid with very fine joints; often used in dressings. (213) Herringbone brickwork *see* Herringbone work.

BROACH *see* SPIRE

BROACH STOP *see* CHAMFER

BROKEN PEDIMENT *see* PEDIMENT

BUCRANIUM. A decorative motif representing the head or skull of an ox, usually garlanded, sometimes found in the metopes of a Doric frieze. (190, 195)

BULL'S EYE WINDOW. A round or oval window, usually with glazing bars radiating from a circular centre. Also called œil-de-bœuf. (135) *See also* Eye, Oculus

BUTMENT *see* ABUTMENT

BUTTERY. In a medieval house, a store-room for food and especially drink, opening on to the screens passage. (184)

BUTTRESS. A mass of masonry or brickwork built against a wall to give it stability or to counteract the outward thrust of an arch or vault behind it. ANGLE BUTTRESS: two buttresses meeting at right angles at the corner of a building. (13) CLASPING BUTTRESS: formed when a solid pier of masonry literally encloses or 'clasps' the external angle of two walls. (10) DIAGONAL BUTTRESS: one placed at the angle formed by the meeting of two perpendicular walls. (11) FLYING BUTTRESS: an arch used to carry the thrust of a vault or roof from the walls of a building to an outer pier or buttress. (14) SETBACK BUTTRESS: two buttresses set back slightly from the corner of a building. (14)

CABLE MOULDING. A convex moulding resembling a cable or rope. Used in Norman architecture. (73, 87)

CABLING. A convex reed-like moulding laid in the flutes of a column, usually decorating about one-third of the shaft from the base upwards. (183)

CAERNARVON ARCH *see* ARCH

CAISSON *see* COFFER

CAMBER. A very slight rise or convex curve in an otherwise horizontal member, such as a beam.

CAMPANILE. A bell tower, usually free-standing. (12)

CANEPHORA *see* CARYATID

CANOPY. A suspended or projecting cover above an altar, tomb, throne or seat, etc. Related to HOOD, which is usually found over a fireplace, niche, door, etc. (91)

CANOPY OF HONOUR *see* CEILURE

CANTILEVER. A structural member which projects beyond the line of support. (215)

CAP. The domical crowning feature of a windmill; the abbreviation for capital.

CAPITAL. The uppermost part of a column or pilaster. (116, 118, 119, 120, 121)

CAROLEAN. A period embracing the reigns of Charles I (1625–49) and Charles II (1660–85). The term is often applied to a comfortable-looking red brick, hipped-roof style, which flourished between 1640 and 1670. (137)

CARTOUCHE. A shaped tablet enclosed in an ornamental frame or scroll and often bearing an inscription or heraldic device. (102, 171)

CARYATID. One of a series of sculptured female figures used instead of columns. When they carry baskets on their heads they are called canephorae. (163) *See also* Atlantes

CASEMENT. A window hinged on one of its edges, so as to open inwards or outwards. In general use until the introduction of the sash window in the seventeenth century. (183) *See also* Sash

CASINO. A temple or a small house, usually within a park. The term is really a generic one and is often synonymous with casina.

CASTELLATED. Decorated like a castle with battlements, turrets, etc. (153)

CASTLE. A fortified building, a place for defence, a stronghold. The evolution of the English castle is essentially a post-Norman development of the earliest Norman castles, consisting of a motte or mound defended by a rampart and ditch and possibly carrying some form of timber superstructure. Later the foot of the mound was extended by a bailey or simple enclosure, itself protected by a rampart or ditch. This type of castle became known as a motte and bailey. The form of a bailey varied considerably and it became the enclosure for hall, chapel, stables, kitchen, etc. Later in the twelfth century, timber superstructures on mottes were replaced by stone keeps — hence the keep and bailey castle; although stone keeps were often raised in place of mottes. In more complete castles, the bailey or ward would itself be defended

13

by a gatehouse and a further outer bailey, thus *inner* and *outer* baileys. The castle as a co-ordinated defence system did not evolve, however, until the very late twelfth and early thirteenth centuries, when new fortification techniques introduced the type of castle surrounded by a curtain wall punctuated at intervals by towers and gatehouses. The scientific system of defence reached its apogee with the concentric castles of Edward I's reign. These were usually quadrangular and symmetrical in plan and were surrounded by an outer system of curtain wall defences. (106, 107) *See also* Arrow loop, Bailey, Barbican, Bartizan, Bastion, Battlements, Curtain wall, Drawbridge, Embrasure, Garderobe, Keep, Machiolation, Moat, Motte, Portcullis, Rampart, Scarp.

CASTLE STYLE. Literally in the style of a castle. Although traceable in origin to some of Vanbrugh's 'toy castles' early in the eighteenth century, the term usually denotes the romantic revival of the picturesque castles in the later eighteenth century. (153)

CATHEDRA. The bishop's throne in a cathedral church.

CAULICOLI. The eight small stalks which spring from the lower stalks or caulis and support the volutes or helix of the Corinthian capital. (120, 123)

CAVETTO. A concave moulding whose profile is usually a quarter of a circle. (118, 121, 197)

CEILURE, CELLURE, CELURE. A panelled and decorated part of a wagon roof, above the rood or altar. Known also as a 'canopy of honour'. (76)

CELL *see* VAULT

CELLA *see* TEMPLE

CENTERING. Temporary framework, usually of timber, to support an arch or vault during construction.

CHAIR-RAIL *see* DADO

CHAMFER. The surface formed when a square angle or arris is cut away obliquely. HOLLOW CHAMFER: one with a concave surface. (68) MOULDED CHAMFER: a moulding replaces the plain surface. (48) STOPPED CHAMFER: a chamfer not carried the length of the piece and finished with a splay or carved stop, sometimes called a broach-stop. (74) SUNK CHAMFER: one with a flat but slightly sunk surface. (79)

CHAMFERED RUSTICATION *see* RUSTICATION

CHANCEL. The eastern part of a parish church, in which the altar is placed. Sometimes separated from the nave by a screen. (8, 9, 75)

CHANCEL ARCH. The arch separating the chancel from the crossing or nave. (75)

CHANCEL SCREEN *see* ROOD SCREEN

CHANTRY CHAPEL. A small chapel within a church, endowed for the saying of masses for the soul of the founder. Often enclosed by tracery screens.

CHAPTER HOUSE. A building attached to a cathedral, collegiate or conventional church and used for the assembly of clergy or chapter. (1, 5)

CHEQUER WORK. An ornamental wall facing achieved by the use of contrasting materials, e.g. knapped flint and stone. (57)

CHEVET. A circular or polygonal apse, surrounded by an ambulatory and radiating chapels. A device common in France, but rarely found in this country. (1, 5, 7)

CHEVRON. A zig-zag moulding, much used in Norman architecture. (66, 73)

CHIMNEY-BREAST. The projection in a room, containing fireplace and flues. (192, 198)

CHIMNEY-CORNER *see* INGLENOOK

CHIMNEY-PIECE. A decorative frame of wood or stone, around the recess in which fuel is burnt. (191, 192, 198)

CHIMNEY-STACK. A structure of masonry or brickwork containing a flue or flues and rising above the roof. (143)

CHINOISERIE. A style incorporating Chinese elements, usually a manifestation of European eighteenth-century Rococo. (199)

CHOIR. The part of a church where services are sung. Occupying the eastern arm and sometimes extending into the nave. Found only in the greater or collegiate churches and cathedrals. (1, 6) *See also* Chancel, Presbytery, Retro-choir, Sanctuary

CHURCH. *See also* Aisle, Altar, Ambulatory, Antependium, Apse, Aumbry, Baldachino, Basilica, Bell-cote, Box pew, Campanile, Canopy, Cathedra, Ceilure, Chancel, Chancel arch, Chantry chapel, Chapter house, Chevet, Choir, Clerestory, Cloister, Crossing, Crypt, Easter Sepulchre, Feretory, Font, Galilee, Hall church, Lady chapel, Lich gate, Low side window, Misericord, Narthex, Nave, Oratory, Parclose, Parvis, Pew, Piscina, Poppy-head, Predella, Presbytery, Priest's door, Pulpit, Pulpitum, Radiating chapels, Reredos, Retable, Retro-choir, Rood loft, Rood screen, Rood stairs, Rose window, Sacristy, Sanctuary, Sedilia, Spire, Spirelet, Squint, Stalls, Steeple, Stoup, Tabernacle, Tabernacle work, Tester, Tracery, Transept, Triforium, Undercroft, Vault, Vestry

CIBORIUM *see* BALDACHINO

CILL *see* SILL

CINCTURE *see* SHAFT RING

CINQUEFOIL *see* FOIL

CIRCUS. In the eighteenth century a circular, or sometimes oval, range of houses, as at John Wood's Circus (1754), Bath.

CLASPING BUTTRESS *see* BUTTRESS

CLASSICISM. A style inspired by ancient Greece and Rome, or at second-hand by the classical trends in Renaissance Italy or southern France.

CLERESTORY, CLEARSTORY. The upper storey of the nave above the aisle roofs, pierced with a series of windows illuminating the interior. (3, 21)

CLOISTER. A covered and often vaulted walk around an open space (usually square on plan), having a plain wall on one side and piers or columns, sometimes filled with tracery on the other. Attached to monasteries, etc. it forms a passageway from the church to the chapter house, refectory and other parts of a monastery. (1)

CLOSE STUDDING *see* STUDS

CLUSTERED COLUMN. A group of several slender shafts joined to form a single column or support. (70)

COADE STONE. An artificial stone manufactured from *c.* 1769 at Lambeth, by Mrs Eleanor Coade, later in partnership with John Sealy. Used for a variety of ornamental purposes. (219)

COB. Clay mixed with chopped straw, gravel and sand. Used as a building material. (217)

COFFER. An ornamental sunk panel in a ceiling or soffit. Also known as a caisson or lacunar. (195)

COIGN *see* QUOIN

COLLAR BEAM *see* ROOF

COLONNADE. A row of columns supporting an entablature. (122, 147)

COLONNETTE. A diminutive column. (89)

COLOSSAL ORDER *see* GIANT ORDER

COLUMBARIUM *see* DOVECOT

COLUMN. A vertical supporting member; in classical architecture consisting of base, shaft and capital. (116)

COLUMNA ROSTRATA, ROSTRAL COLUMN. A column ornamented in the antique style with the projecting beaks of ships' prows. Usually symbolical of naval victory. (103)

COMMON RAFTER *see* ROOF

COMPOSITE ORDER *see* ORDER

COMPOUND PIER *see* PIER

CONGÉ *see* APOPHYGE

CONSOLE. A scrolled bracket. Synonymous with ancon, truss. (200) *See also* Bracket, Corbel, Modillion

COPING. A protective capping or covering to a wall, usually sloping to carry off water. (178)

CORBEL. A supporting projection on the face of a wall, often carved or moulded. (26, 28)

18

CORBELLING. A series of masonry or brick courses, each built out beyond the one below it, to support a chimney stack, oriel window, angle turret, etc. (114)

CORBEL TABLE. A projecting course of masonry, e.g. cornice, parapet, etc. resting on a range of corbels usually connected by small arches. (73)

CORBIE-STEP GABLE *see* GABLE

CORINTHIAN ORDER *see* ORDER

CORNICE. The uppermost member of an entablature, also any moulded projection which crowns or finishes the part to which it is fixed, e.g. a wall, door or window. (116, 117, 118, 119, 120, 121, 201)

CORONA. The projecting member with a flat vertical face, below the cymatium and above the bed mould of a cornice. Its under-surface is generally recessed to form a drip. (117, 118, 119, 120, 121, 122, 123)

COTTAGE ORNÉE. A small building consciously imitating the careless rustic style of the vernacular. A manifestation of the Picturesque. (156)

COUPLE ROOF *see* ROOF

COURSED RUBBLE *see* RUBBLE MASONRY

COURT. An open area, usually enclosed by a wall, in front or behind a building. In Cambridge the term is synonymous with quadrangle. (129) *See also* Quadrangle

COVE, COVING. A large concave moulding, especially between the ceiling of a room and its cornice. (195)

CRADLE ROOF *see* ROOF

CRENEL, CRENELLE *see* BATTLEMENT

CRESCENT. A concave row of houses.

CRESTING. A line of ornament finishing a roof, screen, wall, etc. (78) *See also* Brattishing

CREST TILE. One of a series of ornamental ridge tiles. (16, 218)

CRINKLE CRANKLE. A continuously curving or serpentine wall. Mostly built in the late eighteenth century in Suffolk. (222)

CROCKET, CROCKETING. Carved projections, usually of stylised leaf form, decorating the edges of pinnacles, gables, etc., in Gothic architecture. (86, 90)

CROCKET CAPITAL. A Transitional capital on which a series of crockets have been carved. (68) *See also* Transitional.

CROSSING. The space formed by the intersection of nave, chancel and transepts in a cruciform church. (1)

CROSS VAULT *see* VAULT

CROSS WINDOW. A window with one mullion and one transom

CROW-STEP GABLE *see* GABLE

CROWN. The highest point of an arch or vault. (33, 46) *See also* Vault

CROWN STEEPLE *see* SPIRE

CRUCKS. Pairs of heavy timbers curved inwards from the outer walls to support a ridge beam. Each cruck is called a blade. A form of vernacular construction. (164)

CRYPT. A subterranean chamber in churches, usually beneath the floor of the east end. (31) *See also* Undercroft

CUPOLA. A term used to denote a small domed roof; a small domed turret built upon a roof, and also the inside of a dome. (137)

CURTAIL STEP. The lowest step of a flight of stairs, which projects beyond the newel, finishing in a curve or scroll. (211)

CURTAIN WALL. The outer wall of a castle, connecting towers and gatehouse. Also called enceinte. (106)

CURVILINEAR TRACERY *see* TRACERY

CUSHION CAPITAL. A cubical capital, with the lower angles rounded off. Mostly used in Romanesque and early medieval architecture. (31, 66)

CUSHIONED FRIEZE *see* PULVINATED FRIEZE

CUSP. The point formed by the intersection of two arcs or foils in a Gothic arch or tracery. (63)

CUT STRING *see* STRING

CUTWATER. The wedge-shaped end of the pier of a bridge, which serves to break the current of water.

CYMA. A moulding composed of a double curve. In the CYMA RECTA or OGEE MOULDING, the upper part is concave and the lower, convex. (117, 119, 120, 121, 123, 197) In the CYMA REVERSA, or REVERSE OGEE, the upper part is convex and the lower, concave. Also called a keel moulding. (117, 118, 119, 120, 121, 122, 123)

CYMATIUM. The crowning member of a cornice, generally in the form of a cyma. (118, 119)

D ADO. On the pedestal of an order, the die or that part between the base and the cornice. (201) When the lower portion of a wall is clearly marked off like a base or pedestal, it is also known as a dado. Its capping or surbase is called a D A D O R A I L or chair rail. (200, 203) The base or plinth is commonly called a skirting. *See also* Die, Skirting, Surbase

D A G G E R. A lancet-shaped motif found in tracery of the Decorated style. (62) *See also* Mouchette

D A I S. A platform or place of honour, raised at the end of a room. Originally found in the halls of large medieval and Tudor houses. (184)

D E C A S T Y L E *see* T E M P L E

D E C O R A T E D. A stylistic phase of English Gothic architecture, succeeding the Early English *c.* 1290 and preceding the English Perpendicular *c.* 1360. It is characterised by a change in tracery, at first geometrical, then flowing. (47)

D E M I - C O L U M N. A column half sunk into a wall.

D E N T I L. One of a series of small rectangular blocks arranged like a row of teeth, projecting from the lower part of the Ionic, Corinthian, Composite and sometimes, Doric cornices. (119, 120, 123)

D I A G O N A L B U T T R E S S *see* B U T T R E S S

D I A G O N A L R I B S *see* V A U L T

D I A P E R. An all-over pattern of carved or painted motifs, usually of small square or lozenge shapes. (47)

D I E. That part of a pedestal between the base and cornice. (201) *See also* Dado

DIASTYLE *see* INTERCOLUMNIATION

DIOCLETIAN WINDOW. A semicircular window divided by two upright mullions. The centre portion being larger than the two sides. A Neo-Palladian motif, derived from the Baths of Diocletian. Also called a therm window. (146)

DIPTERAL *see* TEMPLE

DISCHARGING ARCH *see* RELIEVING ARCH

DISTYLE *see* TEMPLE

DODECASTYLE *see* TEMPLE

DOGLEGGED STAIR *see* STAIR

DOG TOOTH. A repeating ornament of four lobes radiating from a raised centre and usually set diagonally upon a moulding. An Early English motif. (43, 68)

DOME. A convex covering, usually hemispherical or semi-elliptical over a circular or polygonal space. A small dome is sometimes called a cupola. (139, 141, 146) *See also* Cupola

DOMICAL VAULT *see* VAULT

DONJON *see* KEEP

DORIC ORDER *see* ORDER

DORMER. An upright window in a projection from the sloping plane of a roof. (134, 137) *See also* Lucarne

DOUBLE-FRAMED ROOF *see* ROOF

DOVECOT. A detached building, usually square or round on plan, the inner face of which is honeycombed with small recesses for nesting. Also known as a columbarium. (127)

DRAWBRIDGE. A bridge over the moat or ditch of castle or fortified town. Hinged at one end and free at the other, it could be raised and lowered at will. (109)

DRESSINGS. Worked and finished stones used on any elevational treatment.

DRIP. A small projection beneath a cornice etc., from which rain-water drips and is thus prevented from flowing back and running down the face of a building. (179) *See also* Throat

DRIPSTONE *see* HOOD MOULD

DROP. The lower projecting end of a newel. (204)

DROP ARCH *see* ARCH

DROPS *see* GUTTAE

DROP TRACERY *see* TRACERY

DRUM. The circular or polygonal wall on which a dome rests. (139, 141, 146) The circular blocks of stone that make up a column. The term is also applied to the solid part or bell of the Corinthian and Composite capitals.

DUTCH GABLE *see* GABLE

EARLY ENGLISH. A stylistic phase of English Gothic architecture covering the thirteenth century. It follows the Norman and precedes the Decorated. A characteristic feature is the lancet window without tracery. (52)

EASTER SEPULCHRE. A recess containing a tomb chest, bearing a representation of the burial and resurrection of Christ; usually placed on the north wall of a chancel. (90)

EAVES. The lower edge of a roof overhanging a wall. The eaves may be left open or finished with a cornice, cove or soffit. (134, 165)

ECHINUS. The convex moulding or ovolo of a capital supporting the abacus. Sometimes enriched with an egg and dart pattern. (117, 118, 122)

EDGE MOULDING *see* ROLL MOULDING

EGG AND ANCHOR, EGG AND DART, EGG AND TONGUE. Patterns of alternating oval and pointed motifs, used to enrich ovolo mouldings. (197)

EGYPTIAN HALL. A hall with an internal peristyle of columns; a compartment described by Vitruvius and interpreted by Palladio, hence its popularity with the English Palladians. That at Holkham, having an apse, is a combination of the classical basilica (as interpreted by Palladio) and the Egyptian hall. (195)

EGYPTIAN REVIVAL. The adaption of Egyptian forms and details resulting from archaeological studies and finding greatest favour around 1800. (162, 195)

ELEVATION. An external front of any building; also a drawing made to show any one face. *See also* Façade

ELIZABETHAN. The architecture of the reign of Queen Elizabeth I (1558–1603), characterised by a naïve interpretation of Renaissance principles of design and ornament, incorporating some late Gothic elements. (130)

ELLIPTICAL ARCH *see* ARCH

EMBATTLED. Furnished with battlements. (61, 129, 171)

EMBRASURE. An opening splayed from within, usually in a fortified building. (180) When applied to the intermediate spaces between merlons it is synonymous with crenelle. *See also* Battlement

ENCAUSTIC TILE. Glazed and decorated earthenware tiles, used for flooring. (100)

ENCEINTE *see* CURTAIN WALL

ENGAGED COLUMN, ATTACHED COLUMN. A column applied or built into a wall. (149)

ENGLISH BOND *see* BRICKWORK

ENTABLATURE. In the classical orders the assembly of horizontal members, architrave, frieze and cornice, supported by a column. (116) These members may also be used on a wall without columnar support.

ENTASIS. A very slight convex curve or swelling on the profile of a column shaft, intended to counteract the optical illusion of concavity. It occurs most frequently in classical architecture and especially Greek architecture.

ENTRESOL *see* MEZZANINE

EQUILATERAL ARCH *see* ARCH

ESCUTCHEON. A shield for armorial bearings. (136)

ETRUSCAN STYLE. A style of decoration inspired by the colouring (black, terracotta and white) of what was believed to be Etruscan (in fact, Greek) pottery. Introduced to England by Robert Adam *c.* 1772. (202)

EUSTYLE *see* INTERCOLUMNIATION

EXEDRA. A large semicircular or angular recess in a wall. (195) *See also* Apse

EXTRADOS. The outer curve of an arch. (194) *See also* Intrados

EXTRUDED CORNERS. A right-angled (or circular) projection from the inner angles of a building around a court or with advancing wings. They usually contain a staircase, or sometimes the oriel of a hall, and are often terminated above the roof-line with an ogee dome. They are mostly to be found as part of sixteenth- or seventeenth-century plans. (130)

EYE. The centre of any part, e.g. the small circle at the centre of a volute; the small window in the centre of a pediment, or the opening in the crown of a dome. (149) *See also* Bull's eye window, Oculus

EYE-CATCHER *see* FOLLY

FAÇADE. The face or front of a building but especially the principal front. *See also* Elevation

FACING. The finishing of the outer surface of a building.

FANLIGHT. Originally the semicircular or fan-shaped window above a door, now used to describe any window above a door. (181, 219)

FAN VAULT *see* VAULT

FASCIA. A long flat member or band, e.g. the horizontal divisions of an architrave; (118, 119, 120, 121) the flat board covering the ends of rafters under the eaves; or the name board over a shop window. (181)

FENESTRATION. A general term applied to the arrangement of windows in a building.

FERETORY. A shrine containing relics, placed behind the high altar; or a room or chapel in which shrines were kept. (1)

FERME ORNÉE. Any farm building ornamented to disguise its utilitarian character. (158)

FESTOON. A carved, modelled or painted garland of flowers, fruit or leaves, suspended in a curve between two points. (191, 192) *See also* Swag

FIELDED PANEL. A panel with a raised central area. (192)

FILLET. A narrow flat band used to separate two mouldings or to terminate a series of mouldings as in a cornice. (70, 117, 118, 121, 197) Sometimes called a listel. Also the flat surface between the flutes in a column. (119, 120)

FINIAL. An ornament crowning a pinnacle, spire, gable, pediment, roof or any other form. The carved tops of bench ends are also called finials. (20)

FIREPLACE. An open recess at the base of a chimney in which fuel is burnt; a hearth. (191)

FLAMBOYANT TRACERY *see* TRACERY

FLÈCHE. A slender wooden spire rising from a roof; sometimes covered with lead. (21)

FLEMISH BOND *see* BRICKWORK

FLEURON. A floral ornament on the centre of the abacus of the Corinthian capital. (120) The term is sometimes loosely applied to medieval decoration as well.

FLOWING TRACERY *see* TRACERY

FLUSHWORK. The use of flint and dressed stone to produce decorative wall patterns. Indigenous to East Anglia. (216) *See also* Knapped flint

FLUTES, FLUTING. The vertical grooves on the shaft of a column, pilaster or other surface. Of semicircular, segmental or semi-elliptical section, the flutes may meet in an arris or be separated by a fillet. Also called striges. (120)

FLYING BUTTRESS *see* BUTTRESS

FOIL. Each of the small arc openings in Gothic tracery separated by cusps. Trefoil (three), quatrefoil (four), cinquefoil (five), express the number of foils. (43, 46, 63, 86)

FOLIATED. Any surface covered with leaf ornament.

FOLLY. An architectural joke, or a nonconforming and sometimes fantastic structure in a parkscape. The term is usually synonymous with eye-catcher. (155)

FONT. A vessel to contain the water used in baptism. Usually placed near the west end of a church. It may be of stone or, more rarely, lead. (87)

FORMERETS *see* VAULT

FORTRESS *see* CASTLE

FOSSE. A ditch or moat. (112)

FOUR-CENTRED TUDOR ARCH *see* ARCH

FRATER *see* REFECTORY

FRENCH WINDOW. A window that opens to floor level in two leaves like a pair of doors.

FRET. An ornamental pattern of repeated combinations of straight vertical and horizontal lines. Also called Greek key pattern. (177, 195)

FRIEZE. That part of an entablature between the architrave and the cornice; or any similar decorative band or feature. (116, 117, 118, 119, 120, 121, 122, 123)

FRONTISPIECE. The principal façade or bay of a building.

FROSTED *see* RUSTICATION

GABLE. The triangular portion of wall at the end of a ridge roof. SHAPED GABLE: one with multi-curved sides. (133) DUTCH GABLE: a curved or shaped gable surmounted by a pediment. (135) CROW-STEP or CORBIE-STEP GABLE: one with stepped sides. (125) HIPPED GABLE: a gable with the uppermost part sloped back.

GABLET. A small gable used ornamentally on a buttress, over a niche, in woodwork, etc. (18)

GADROON. A decorative pattern formed of a series of convex ridges. (104)

GALILEE. A vestibule or chapel enclosing a porch at the west end of a church, as at Ely, Durham and Lincoln. (82)

GALLERY. In Elizabethan and Jacobean houses, a long room or 'long gallery', usually on an upper floor and extending the whole length of the house. (185) In a church, an upper storey above the aisle, arched to the nave and sometimes called the tribune but not the clerestory or triforium. Also, a projecting platform or balcony in a church or theatre; in Tudor halls called the minstrel gallery. (188) Lastly, a room or separate building used to display pictures and sculpture.

GALLETING, GARRETING. The insertion of tiny pieces of stone or flint into mortar courses while still soft. (49)

GAMBREL ROOF *see* ROOF

GARDEROBE. Euphemism for a privy in a medieval castle. Built, either within the thickness of the castle wall, or else projecting beyond the wall. It drained into the moat or into a special pit. (114)

GARGOYLE. A spout in the form of a carved grotesque human or animal head, projecting from the top of a wall, to throw off rainwater. (83)

GARRETING *see* GALLETING

GAUGED BRICKWORK *see* BRICKWORK

GAZEBO. A look-out tower or elevated summer-house which commands a view. Often incorporated in a garden wall. (144) *See also* Belvedere

GEOMETRICAL STAIR *see* STAIR

GEOMETRICAL TRACERY *see* TRACERY

GEORGIAN. Generally, the period of the reign of the four Georges (1714–1830). More particularly in architecture, the style of the Neo-Palladians and their successors before the Regency. (147, 148, 149, 150, 151)

GIANT ORDER. A column or pilaster extending over two or more storeys of a building. Sometimes called a colossal order. (142)

GIBBS SURROUND. A window or door with a triple keystoned head beneath a cornice, and blocks of stone punctuating the jambs. Popularised by James Gibbs. (173)

GLYPHS *see* TRIGLYPHS

GOTHIC. In England, the style of architecture succeeding the Norman or Romanesque and subdivided chronologically and stylistically into several periods (Early English, Decorated, Perpendicular). It may be generally characterised by the use of the pointed arch and the vault.

GOTHIC REVIVAL. A deliberate attempt to recreate the decoration and atmosphere of Gothic architecture. The eighteenth-century 'Gothick' was initiated by William Kent *c*. 1730, and had as its most famous apologist Horace Walpole *c*. 1755. The revival was undertaken with much more seriousness and scholarship in the nineteenth century. It is not to be confused with the survival of Gothic forms in provincial building. (152, 154)

GREEK KEY *see* FRET

GREEK REVIVAL. The interest in Greece as a source for architectural style is an archaeological manifestation. The beginnings of the Revival in England may be traced back to 1755 and the return of James Stuart and Nicholas Revett from their Greek explorations. Although the first volume of their *Antiquities of Athens* appeared in 1762, and the second in 1788, by which time many other Greek surveys had been published, for most of the century Greece was a source only for ornament or garden structures. Not until about 1800, in the hands of architects such as William Wilkins, did English building capture something of the Greek sense of mass and siting. (163)

GROIN *see* VAULT

GROTESQUE. A form of decoration composed of fanciful animal and human forms, fruit, flowers, etc. (190) *See also* Arabesque

GROTTO. An artificial cave, often decorated with stalactites and shells, sometimes providing a setting for sculpture, fountains, etc. Frequently found in eighteenth-century English parks. (157)

GUILLOCHE. A repeating pattern of interlaced spirals. Used to ornament mouldings. (193)

GUTTAE. Small 'drops' or conic projections under the mutules and triglyphs of a Doric entablature. (118)

Hagioscope *see* SQUINT

HALF-HIPPED ROOF *see* ROOF

HALF-TIMBER CONSTRUCTION *see* TIMBER FRAMING

HALL. The first room on entering a house. In medieval houses and colleges also the communal room entered at the lower end through screens and screens passage, and having at the upper end a dais usually lit by a bay window. In later architecture the hall was situated on a central axis, where it became a vestibule communicating with other parts of the house. (184, 188, 194)

HALL CHURCH. A church with nave and aisles of the same height. (41)

HAMMER BEAM *see* ROOF

HAUNCH. The part of an arch between the crown and the springing. (46)

HEADER *see* BRICKWORK

HEADING BOND *see* BRICKWORK

HELIX. One of the small spirals or volutes under the abacus of the Corinthian capital. (120, 123)

HELM ROOF *see* SPIRE

HERM *see* TERM

HERRINGBONE WORK. An arrangement of bricks, stone, tiles or wood blocks, laid diagonally to form a zig-zag pattern on a floor or wall. (212)

HERTFORDSHIRE SPIKE *see* SPIRE

HEXASTYLE *see* TEMPLE

HIP. The external angle formed by the intersection of the sloping sides of a roof.

HIPPED GABLE *see* GABLE

HIPPED ROOF *see* ROOF

HOLLOW CHAMFER *see* CHAMFER

HOOD *see* CANOPY

HOOD-MOULD. In medieval archite *ture, a projecting moulding over an opening to throw off rain-water; (48, 83) also known as a dripstone or, when rectangular, a label. (129) A LABEL STOP is an ornamental boss terminating a label or hood-mould. (48, 83)

HORSESHOE ARCH *see* ARCH

IMPOST. The member, usually moulded, on which the ends of an arch rest. (43)

INGLENOOK. A recess, usually with a bench or seat, flanking a fireplace. May be called a chimney-corner.

INTERCOLUMNIATION. The space between two columns, measured at the lower part of their shaft. The formula for this spacing varies. PYCNO-STYLE: the spacing of columns $1\frac{1}{2}$ diameters apart. This is close spacing. SYSTYLE: columns spaced 2 diameters apart. EUSTYLE: columns spaced $2\frac{1}{4}$ diameters apart. DIASTYLE: the spacing of columns $2\frac{3}{4}$ to 4 diameters apart. ARAEOSTYLE: columns spaced at more than 3 diameters apart. The Eustyle is the most common.

INTERSECTED TRACERY *see* TRACERY

INTRADOS. The inner curve or underside of an arch; also known as a soffit. (194) *See also* Extrados

IONIC ORDER *see* ORDER

JACOBEAN. A style of architecture predominant during the reign of James I (1603–25); a logical development from the Elizabethan style but characterised by an increasing awareness of purer classical forms, and in its later development influenced by the classicising of Inigo Jones. (131)

JAMB. The vertical side of a doorway, window, archway or fireplace opening. (42, 219)

JETTY *see* OVERHANG

JIB DOOR. A concealed internal door, flush with the wall and constructed so as to appear part of the wall surface.

JOIST. One of several parallel beams upon which floor boards or ceiling laths are fastened. (45, 180)

Keel MOULDING *see* CYMA

KEEP. The massive inner tower or stronghold of a castle, sometimes called a donjon. (110) The term, dungeon, is said to be derived from the underground cells of a donjon. A SHELL KEEP which first appeared in the late eleventh century, consists of a buttressed curtain wall at the top of a conical motte. (112)

KENTISH TRACERY *see* TRACERY

KEY PATTERN *see* FRET

KEYSTONE. The central wedge-shaped block or voussoir of an arch, which locks the whole together. Keystones are also used as ornaments on the heads of doors and windows. (173, 219)

KING POST *see* ROOF

KNAPPED FLINT. Flints cut and laid so that their split sides form a smooth black facing to a wall. Often set in patterns. (216) *See also* Flushwork

KNEELER. A short piece of the coping to a gable, bonded into the wall.

LABEL *see* HOOD-MOULD

LABEL STOP *see* HOOD-MOULD

LACUNAR *see* COFFER

LADY CHAPEL. A chapel dedicated to the Blessed Virgin. Usually placed behind the high altar, at the east end of a church.

LANCET. A tall narrow pointed window, characteristic of Early English architecture. Often grouped in threes, fives or sevens at the east end of a church. (52)

LANCET ARCH *see* ARCH

LANTERN. A small circular or polygonal structure raised on a dome or roof in order to admit light. (134, 139, 141) Also applied to that stage of a central tower of a church, containing windows to light the crossing. (18)

LATTICE. An openwork screen composed of criss-crossed metal or wooden members. (190) Also, a window with diamond-shaped leaded lights. (218)

LEAN-TO ROOF *see* ROOF

LEPER'S WINDOW *see* LOW SIDE WINDOW

LESENE. A pilaster without base or capital. Also called pilaster strip. (72)

LICH GATE, LYCH GATE. A covered gateway, usually of wood, placed at the entrance to a churchyard, where, during a funeral, the coffin could be set down until the clergyman arrived. (99)

LIERNE RIBS *see* VAULT

LIERNE VAULT *see* VAULT

LIGHTS *see* MULLION

LINENFOLD PANELLING. A form of carved panelling, ornamented with a conventional representation of vertically folded linen. Frequently found in fifteenth- and sixteenth-century interiors. (93)

LINTEL. The horizontal member that spans an opening. (214)

LISTEL *see* FILLET

LOGGIA. A covered colonnade or arcade open to the air on at least one side. (159)

LONG AND SHORT WORK. In Saxon architecture, a method of laying quoins, in which flat horizontal slabs alternate with tall vertical ones. Also used as a bonding device for lesenes. (72)

LONG GALLERY *see* GALLERY

LOOK-OUT TOWER *see* BELVEDERE

LOOPHOLE, LOOP WINDOW. A vertical slot in a wall for air and light. (19) *See also* Arrow loop, loophole

LOUVER, LOUVRE, LUFFER. A ventilator in the form of a turret or lantern on the roof of a medieval hall or kitchen. (124) Also, a series of inclined overlapping boards or slats, fixed horizontally to admit air but exclude rain. (16)

LOWSIDE WINDOW. A window usually in the chancel south wall, perhaps for outside communicants or for a sanctus bell. Frequently called a Leper's Window.

LOZENGE. A diamond-shaped panel or figure with four equal sides. (64)

LUCARNE. A small window, usually projecting from a sloping roof, e.g. on the face of a Gothic spire, when it may be capped by a gablet and finial. (18) *See also* Dormer

LUNETTE. A semicircular window or panel. (138)

LYCH GATE *see* LICH GATE

MACHICOLATION. A projecting parapet on a castle wall or tower, having openings in the floor between the supporting corbels, through which missiles, etc. could be dropped on the enemy. (107, 114)

MANDORLA *see* VESICA PISCIS

MANOR HOUSE. A generic term applied to the principal house of a manor or village; more specifically it refers to a late medieval, unfortified house.

MANSARD ROOF *see* ROOF

MANTEL, MANTELSHELF. The shelf above a mantelpiece or chimney-piece. Although Gwilt's *Encyclopaedia of Architecture* defines mantelpiece as the horizontal decoration above the opening, modern usage applies the term, like chimney-piece, to the whole ornamental surround. (201) *See also* Chimney-piece

MASONRY *see* RUBBLE MASONRY

MAUSOLEUM. A building designed to contain one or more tombs. (162)

MEDALLION. A round or oval plaque bearing a carved or painted representation of a figure or other subject. (199)

MERLON *see* BATTLEMENT

METOPE. The plain or decorated space between the triglyphs in a Doric frieze. (118)

MEWS. Originally where hawks were kept, but after the seventeenth century referring to the stabling of horses. In domestic planning behind town houses with minor accommodation above the stables.

MEZZANINE. An intermediate storey between two floors. Also called an entresol. (150)

MINSTREL GALLERY *see* GALLERY

MISERICORD. A bracket on the underside of a hinged choir stall seat, which when the seat is turned up gives support during long periods of standing. Often carved with animal and allegorical figures. Sometimes called a miserere. (96)

MITRE. In joinery, the diagonal joint formed by the meeting of two mouldings of the same section at right angles. (197)

MOAT. A deep, wide ditch surrounding a castle, house or town and usually filled with water. (106, 107)

MODILLION. One of a series of blocks or brackets under the corona of the Corinthian and Composite orders. The term is sometimes loosely applied to the consoles or brackets supporting a cornice. (123, 193, 199)

MODULE. A unit of measure (usually half the diameter and sometimes the diameter of a column at the base of its shaft), by which the proportions of the parts of an order or building are regulated. The module, if half the diameter, is divided into thirty minutes or parts, and if a full diameter, into sixty minutes. (118, 120)

MOTTE. A steep truncated mound of earth, forming the dominant feature and stronghold of a Norman castle. It was surrounded by a deep ditch and its flattened top was fortified by a timber stockade and tower. Although it may stand alone, it was generally accompanied by one or more baileys, hence the term motte and bailey castle. (112) *See also* Castle

MOUCHETTE. A curved dagger motif, found in tracery of the curvilinear style. (63) *See also* Dagger

MOULDED CHAMFER *see* CHAMFER

MOULDINGS. Projecting or recessed bands used to ornament a wall or other surface; they may be plain or enriched. Each style of architecture produces its own characteristic mouldings.

MULLION. A vertical member dividing a window into 'lights', each of which may be further sub-divided into panes. The crudest form is the baluster mullion of Anglo-Saxon churches. (61, 137, 169) *See also* Transom

MUNTIN. The intermediate member or stile in the framing of a panelled door, screen, etc., as distinct from the horizontal member or members called rails. (187) *See also* Rail, Stile

MUTULE. One of a series of projecting inclined blocks under the corona of a Doric cornice and over each triglyph. Sometimes hung with guttae. (118)

NAILHEAD. An ornament in the shape of a small pyramidal stud resembling a nail head. Usually employed as a repeating motif in late Norman and Early English architecture. (70)

NARTHEX. A vestibule or portico stretching across the main entrance of a church.

NAVE. The main body or central aisle of a church, extending from the entrance to the transepts, or, if there are no transepts, to the choir or chancel. (1, 2, 3, 4, 8, 9)

NECK, NECKING. The space between the lowest annulet of the capital and the astragal of the shaft of a Doric order. (117, 118, 122)

NEEDLE SPIRE *see* SPIRE

NEO-CLASSICAL. The style of architecture and decoration which dominated virtually all of Europe from about 1760 to 1790. It is the product of the new archaeological and eclectic attitude towards antiquity as a source for modern invention, formulated in France and Italy in the 1750s. Unlike their predecessors who accepted traditional text book views of antiquity, artists of the new generation devoted themselves to first-hand investigation of the monuments themselves, not only in Rome, but also in the newly excavated cities of Herculaneum and Pompeii, in Paestum, Asia Minor, Greece and other outposts of ancient civilisation. They looked upon the material they found, not as models for slavish imitation, but as a storehouse from which to create a new classical style using the same logic, judgement and imagination that had directed the ancients. In England, the leading exponents of the style were Robert Adam, James 'Athenian' Stuart and Sir William Chambers. (193, 200, 201)

NEWEL. The central pillar from which the steps of a winding stair radiate. Also the principal post at the angles of a square staircase which supports the string and handrail. (209) *See also* Drop

NEWEL STAIR *see* STAIR

NICHE. A recess in a wall, pier, etc., usually semicircular and arched, to receive a statue, urn or other object. (136)

NOGGING. The use of brickwork, stone, etc. to fill in the spaces between the studs or uprights in a timber-framed building. (168)

NORMAN. The post-Conquest style current during the eleventh and twelfth centuries in England, preceding the Gothic and following the Saxon. Roughly synonymous with the European term, Romanesque. (31, 42, 43, 44, 66)

NOSING. The rounded edge of a tread, projecting above the riser. Also applied to any projecting rounded edge. (210, 211)

OBELISK. A tall four-sided tapering shaft with a pyramidal top. (145)

OCTASTYLE *see* TEMPLE

OCULUS. Any small round or oval window. (143) *See also* Bull's eye window, Eye

ŒIL-DE-BŒUF *see* BULL'S EYE WINDOW

OFF-SET *see* WEATHERING

OGEE ARCH *see* ARCH

OGEE MOULDING *see* CYMA

OPEN NEWEL STAIR *see* STAIR

OPEN PEDIMENT *see* PEDIMENT

OPEN WELL STAIR *see* STAIR

OPTICAL REFINEMENT *see* ENTASIS

ORANGERY. A gallery or building in which orange trees and other plants are cultivated. Introduced in this country in the seventeenth century, it usually has a range of large tall windows on the south side. (151)

ORATORY. A small chapel or room for private devotions and prayer.

ORDER. The essential components of a complete order are a column with base, shaft and capital and an entablature with architrave, frieze and cornice. A pedestal may be added but it is not an essential part. The size and proportions of these parts varies with each order. The three Greek orders are: Doric, Ionic and Corinthian. To these the Romans added two more — Tuscan and Composite. The TUSCAN, a simplified Doric is the plainest and most massive of the five. (116, 117) The DORIC is primarily distinguished by the triglyphs and metopes in its frieze and the mutules under its corona. The Greek Doric has no base and a fluted shaft, (50) while the Roman has a base and a fluted or unfluted shaft. (116, 118) The IONIC is characterised by the volutes of its capital and the dentils in its cornice. Its shaft is generally fluted and its base Attic. (116, 119) The CORINTHIAN differs from the Doric mainly by its bell-shaped capital ornamented with acanthus, olive or laurel leaves, from which eight small volutes or caulicoli emerge. Its shaft is normally fluted. (116, 120, 123) The COMPOSITE or ROMAN is the most elaborate of the five orders and the one which admits the most variations. Its capital combines the volutes of the Ionic with the foliate bell of the Corinthian. (116, 121)

ORIEL WINDOW. A bay window projecting from an upper storey, supported upon corbels. (125)

OUTER STRING *see* STRING

OVERDOOR. A decorative painting or bas-relief placed above a door and usually forming part of the door-case. Also called a sopraporte. (196)

OVERHANG. The projecting upper storey of a building. In a timber-framed building the projection of floor joists is called a jetty. (168, 169) Also used to describe eaves which project beyond the top of a wall. (159, 214)

OVERSAILING COURSE. Courses of stone or brick where each course projects beyond the one below. (125)

OVOLO. A convex moulding usually a quarter of a circle and sometimes ornamented with egg and dart or similar motifs. (117, 118, 119, 120, 121, 122)

ℙ︁AD STONE *see* TEMPLATE

PALLADIAN. The architecture of Andrea Palladio and later sixteenth-century Venice and the Veneto, particularly of Vicenza. Introduced to England by Inigo Jones in 1615, it remained a Court style. When revived as a Jones-Palladio revival early in the eighteenth century by Colin Campbell and Lord Burlington, etc. it became a national style. (147, 175)

PALLADIAN MOTIF. An arch over columns whose entablatures span narrower side openings; the whole of this tripartite motif framed by the columns or pilasters of a superior order. Famous from Palladio's Basilica at Vicenza. (175) *See also* Venetian window

PALMETTE. A conventionalised ornament resembling the fan-shaped palm (or palmetto) leaf. Alternating with lotus, it forms the classical anthemion pattern. The single palmette, of which there are numerous variations, is frequently called honeysuckle or anthemion. (200) *See also* Anthemion

PANELLING. A series of thin sheets of wood (panels) framed together by thicker vertical and horizontal strips of wood, to form a screen or a wooden lining to a room. (187) *See also* Fielded panel, Linenfold panelling, Muntin, Rail, Stile

PANEL TRACERY *see* TRACERY

PANES *see* MULLION

PANTILE. A roof tile of undulating section. (83)

PARAPET. A low protective wall on a bridge, gallery, balcony or above the cornice of a building. On some Jacobean and later houses, the parapet was formed of stone letters, spelling out a motto, date, etc. Later parapets often had open panels filled by balusters. In castles, parapets were battlemented. (111, 136, 143)

PARCLOSE. A screen separating a chapel or tomb from the body of a church. (81)

PARGETTING. A form of plasterwork incised or modelled with ornamental patterns, used to decorate the exteriors of half-timbered houses, during the sixteenth and seventeenth centuries. (218)

PARVIS. A term generally, but wrongly, applied to a room over a church porch. It is really synonymous with porch, in the sense of an enclosed area preceding the entry to a church. (83)

PATERA. A circular or oval disc-like ornament, usually rendered in a low relief. (123, 177) *See also* Rosette

PAVILION. A pleasure house in a park or garden, not in the form of a temple. One of a group of buildings attached by wings to a main block; also, the part projecting from the centre and/or ends of a building. (135, 154)

PEDESTAL. A support for a column, statue, urn, etc. When detailed according to the orders, it consists of a plinth (or base), a die (or dado) and a cap (or cornice). (142)

PEDIMENT. A low-pitched triangular gable usually above an entablature, and finishing the end or ends of a sloping roof. (141, 193) It is used as an ornamental feature above doors and windows, etc. when it may take a variety of forms. BROKEN: when the base of the triangle is left open. (172) OPEN: when the top of the pediment is opened. (144, 191, 193) SEGMENTAL: when tangential in shape. (193) A SCROLLED pediment is an open segmental one, where the ends are scrolled inwards. There are also examples in England of pediments adopting the freer and more mannered forms of the Italian Baroque — particularly of Borromini.

PEEL, PELE. A massive, square, fortified tower, not unlike a keep. Generally built in the border counties of England and Scotland until the sixteenth century. (115)

PENDANT. A form of elongated boss, projecting downwards or suspended from a fan vault (40), Jacobean ceiling (185) or open timber roof.

PENDENTIVE. Each of the spherical concave triangles or spandrels formed by the intersection of a hemispherical dome by two pairs of opposite arches. (194)

PERIPTERAL *see* TEMPLE

PERISTYLE *see* TEMPLE

PERPENDICULAR. The period of English Gothic architecture succeeding the Decorated, *c.* 1335 and preceding the Tudor period, *c.* 1530. Characterised by the strong vertical lines of its tracery. (8, 9, 61)

PERPENDICULAR TRACERY *see* TRACERY

PERRON. A platform or landing immediately preceding the entrance of a building and usually at the head of a flight of steps, to which the term may also be applied. (134)

PERSIANS *see* ATLANTES

PEW. A fixed wooden seat in a church, partially enclosed to the aisles with bench-ends, often terminating in finials called poppyheads.

PIANO NOBILE. In a Renaissance building, the principal storey raised above ground level, containing the reception rooms. (146)

PIAZZA. An open public space surrounded by buildings. 'Very frequently and very ignorantly used to indicate a walk under an arcade'. Gwilt.

PICTURESQUE. The real Picturesque inaugurated in 1794 by Richard Payne Knight's *The Landscape of a Didactic Poem* and Uvedale Price's *Essay on the Picturesque*, is a category of aesthetics distinguished from the Beautiful and the Sublime primarily by qualities of smallness and irregularity. It is mainly concerned with landscape and when applied to architecture refers more to the total appearance of a building in its setting than to its style or stylistic details. Nevertheless, in the hands of men like Nash and Repton, a Picturesque style of architecture, limited to small domestic buildings, especially villas and cottages, was evolved. Its major attributes are, irregularity of plan and profile, and a preference for the 'Castellated', Gothic and Italian or 'Old English' vernacular styles. (159)

PIER. A solid support, usually square in section, employed to sustain the dead load from a beam, lintel or thrust of an arch. (147) In Gothic architecture, a collection of shafts is known as a COMPOUND PIER. (171)

PILASTER. A rectangular column projecting slightly from a wall. In Classical architecture it conforms with the design of the orders. (144)

PILASTER STRIP see LESENE

PILLAR. A detached upright support deviating in shape and proportion from the orders. (44)

PILLAR PISCINA see PISCINA

PINNACLE. A pyramidal or conical ornament used to terminate a gable, buttress, etc. Often decorated with crockets. (20)

PISCINA. A shallow basin with a drain, in which Communion or Mass vessels are washed. Generally placed in a niche, south of the altar. (89) When freestanding on a pillar, it is called a PILLAR PISCINA.

PLATE TRACERY see TRACERY

PLATFORM. A balustraded walk or terrace on top of a building, or any raised level surface. (134)

PLINTH. The lowest projecting member of the base of a column or pedestal. (117, 118, 119, 120, 121) Also the projecting base or skirting of a wall or any other structure. (201)

PLINTH BLOCK. A slightly projecting block at the foot of the architrave of a door, chimney-piece, etc., against which the skirting is stopped. Also called an architrave block or skirting block. (198, 200)

PLOUGHSHARE VAULT *see* VAULT

PODIUM. A continuous pedestal or base to a building. (141) *See also* Stylobate

POINTED ARCH *see* ARCH

POINTING, RE-POINTING. The mortar finish to brick jointing. In old brickwork, the replacing of decayed mortar with new. (212, 214)

POPPYHEAD. The ornamental finial of a bench end, often carved with animals, figures, foliage, etc. (95) *See also* Pew

PORCH. A covered entrance to a building. (1, 2, 3, 4, 83, 163, 165) Internal porches are sometimes to be found in sixteenth-century houses. (187)

PORTAL. Any imposing entrance. (136)

PORTCULLIS. A heavy iron or wooden grating, constructed to slide vertically in grooves cut at the sides of the gateway of a medieval castle, as a defence against assault. (108)

PORTE-COCHÈRE. A porch, very often a portico, large enough to admit a carriage. The term can also refer to the enclosed entrance courtyard, usually of a town house.

PORTICO. A covered colonnade forming an entrance to a building; (141) if projecting from the building it is PROSTYLE, (140) if recessed, IN ANTIS. (148) *See also* Temple

POST CONQUEST ARCHITECTURE *see* NORMAN ARCHITECTURE

POSTERN. A small secondary entrance, usually at the rear of a building. (107)

PREDELLA. The step or platform on which the altar stands; also the ledge or shelf at the back of the altar on which the altar-piece or reredos (if there is one) is placed; and most commonly, the painting or sculpture on the face of this shelf, sometimes forming an appendage to the altar-piece above. In modern art historical usage the term generally refers to any painted or carved appendage to the base of an altar-piece, whether it belongs to the altar-piece or to the shelf which supports it. (80)

PRESBYTERY. That part in the eastern arm of a church between the choir and the sanctuary (i.e. high altar), usually reserved for the clergy. (1) *See also* Chancel, Choir, Sanctuary

PRIEST'S DOOR. A small door leading into the chancel, usually on the south side of a church. (21)

PRINCIPAL RAFTER *see* ROOF

PRINT ROOM. A room for the storage of a print collection, but in the eighteenth century the term was applied to a room decorated with an all-over pattern of prints. A well-known example is at Woodhall House, Hertfordshire, by Thomas Leverton, 1780. (203)

PROFILE. Any section of a moulding.

PROSTYLE *see* PORTICO, TEMPLE

PROTECTORATE STYLE. At its best a competent classical style (Thorpe Hall), expressed in the country house architecture of the decade 1650–60. In its final form it was powerfully influenced by the Dutch manner of Philip Vingboon's book *Gronden . . . Gebouwen*, 1648. It is derived from Artisan Mannerism, a term invented by Sir John Summerson for the anti-court style of the 1630s which was essentially a builder's rather than an architect's creation, characterised by the use of brick and often by an idiosyncratic use of a type of half-pilaster dependent from a shouldered architrave and scrolled at its base. The style appears to have originated in the City of London and to have spread outwards through the Home Counties. (170)

PSEUDODIPTERAL *see* TEMPLE

PSEUDOPERIPTERAL *see* TEMPLE

PULPIT. A raised and enclosed platform from which the sermon is preached. (92)

PULPITUM. A screen, usually of stone, supporting a gallery between the nave and ritual choir of a cathedral or greater church. It might support the rood and frequently the organ for singers. The west face would form a reredos for the parochial altar in the nave. (78) *See also* Rood loft, Rood screen

PULVINATED FRIEZE. A frieze with a convex face. Sometimes called a swelled or cushioned frieze. (182)

PURLIN *see* ROOF

PUTTO. A painted or carved representation of a small naked boy. (102)

PYCNOSTYLE *see* INTERCOLUMNIATION

PYRAMID. A structure with a square or polygonal base and sloping sides meeting at an apex. (162)

QUADRANGLE. An inner square, rectangular space or courtyard of a building. (129) *See also* Court

QUADRIPARTITE VAULT *see* VAULT

QUARRY, QUARREL. A square or diamond-shaped piece of glass leaded into a stained glass window. (58)

QUARRY, QUARRY TILE. A small square clay paving tile.

QUATREFOIL *see* FOIL

QUEEN ANNE STYLE. Queen Anne's reign (1702–14) saw the apogee of Wren and the rise of the English Baroque. (Vanbrugh, Hawksmoor, Archer, etc.) The term is usually applied to a development of domestic Carolean forms, principally executed in red brick. The sash window is habitual, and hipped roofs are frequently disguised behind parapets. (143)

QUEEN POST *see* ROOF

QUIRK. An acute V-shaped groove, often found between a convex moulding and a flat member. Also used to afford shadow to an ogee or ovolo. (68)

QUOIN, COIGN. The external angles of a building and the rusticated or otherwise emphasised stones applied to the angles. (135)

RABBET *see* REBATE

RADIATING CHAPELS. The chapels radiating from the apse or ambulatory of a church. (1)

RAFTER *see* ROOF

RAIL. A horizontal member separating the compartments of a panelled door, screen, wall, etc.; (187) or framing the balusters in a balustrade, (193) or the vertical posts of a fence. *See also* Muntin, Stile

RAINWATER HEAD. A metal container at the top of a rainwater pipe to collect the outflow from a roof gutter. Often beautifully decorated. (53, 179)

RAMP. An inclined plane connecting two different levels. The steep concave slope joining the handrail of a stair to the newel. (211) Also, a sloping shoulder connecting two levels in the coping of a wall. (178)

RAMPART. A protective earth or stone wall, with or without a parapet, surrounding a castle or fortified place. (111)

RAMPART WALK. The footpath on the inside of a rampart. (111)

RANDOM RUBBLE *see* RUBBLE MASONRY

REBATE, RABBET. A groove cut on the edge of a board to receive the edge of another board, specifically of doors and windows.

RECTILINEAR TRACERY *see* TRACERY

REEDING. A form of surface decoration, consisting of a series of parallel convex mouldings placed together; the reverse of fluting. (187)

REFECTORY. The dining hall of a monastery or college, sometimes called the frater.

REGENCY. The style is characterised by chaste and elegant details, and is typified in the familiar bowed and balconied terraces of Brighton, Cheltenham, etc. The Regency style is also widely eclectic, witnessing the rise of the more exotic revivals. Nash's Brighton Pavilion is therefore just as typical of the Regency as are his Regent's Park terraces. (161)

REGULA. The band beneath the tenia in a Doric architrave, to which the guttae are attached. (118)

RELIEVING ARCH. A plain arch built into the wall above a true arch or lintel, to relieve it of some of the load and thrust. Also called a discharging arch.

RENDERING. A coat of mortar or stucco applied to an external wall. The first coat of plaster on an internal wall. (160)

REREDOS. An ornamental structure or screen of stone or wood, covering the wall behind and above an altar. (80)

RESPOND. A half-pillar or similar shaft, or corbel, engaged in a wall to support an arch, usually at the end of an arcade. (66)

RETABLE. An altar-piece or picture, etc., behind but attached to an altar. It also refers to the shelf between the altar and the east wall. (93)

RETAINING WALL. A wall built to retain a bank or hold back a mass of earth, water, etc. Also called a revetment. (137)

RETICULATED TRACERY *see* **TRACERY**

RETRO-CHOIR. The area behind the high altar in a major church.

RETURN. The part of a wall or continuous moulding, frieze, cornice, etc. which turns away (usually at right angles) from the previous direction. (183)

REVEAL. The inside surface, usually of a door or window, cut at right angles to the face of the wall etc. If cut diagonally it can be a splay. (182) *See also* Splay

REVERSE OGEE *see* **CYMA**

REVETMENT *see* RETAINING WALL

RIBS *see* VAULT

RIDGE *see* ROOF

RIDGE RIB *see* VAULT

RISE. Of an arch, the height from the springing line to the crown. Of a stair, the height from one landing to the next and from one tread to the next. Of a roof, the height from the lowest to the highest point.

RISER. In a staircase, the vertical part between the two treads of a stair. (210, 211) *See also* Tread

ROCK FACED *see* RUSTICATION

ROCOCO. A phase of decoration in England, parallel with the later phase of Palladianism and preceding Neo-Classicism. It is essentially an interior style, expressed in fanciful forms, in plasterwork, chimney-pieces and furniture, etc. (171)

ROLL MOULDING. A plain round moulding of semicircular or more than semicircular section. (70, 71) With a fillet, it is a ROLL AND FILLET MOULDING. (67, 70) Used in Early English and Decorated architecture, in Norman architecture it is known as a BOWTELL.

ROMANESQUE *see* NORMAN

ROMAN ORDER *see* ORDER

ROOD LOFT. A gallery on which the 'rood' or crucifix is placed; built over the wood screen, and used on special occasions by minstrels and singers. Hence also called a singing gallery. (77)

ROOD SCREEN. A screen at the west end of the chancel, separating nave and choir and built below the loft (rood loft) on which the rood or crucifix was placed. With the disappearance of the rood and rood loft the screen became synonymous with chancel screen. (77)

ROOD STAIRS. A small staircase giving access to the rood loft, built into the chancel wall or in a special turret. (74)

ROOF. A cover over a building. Types of roof include: LEAN-TO: a roof with a single slope, built against a vertical wall. (22, 166) COUPLE ROOF: a simple roof formed of pairs of rafters (or couples) joined at the apex without tie beams or collar beams. (23) SINGLE FRAMED: a roof without longitudinal members (i.e. ridge beams, purlins, etc.) and consisting only of transverse members. (27) DOUBLE FRAMED: a roof, in which longitudinal members are used. HIPPED: a roof where the ends are sloped inwards instead of being gabled. (137) HALF-HIPPED: when the ends are partly gabled and partly sloped. (165) MANSARD: a roof with two contiguous slopes, where the lower is steeper than the upper. (167) GAMBREL: a form of curved mansard with a ridge gable. (166) WAGON: so called because of its resemblance to the stretched canvas roof of a wagon. Formed by closely set rafters with arched braces and often panelled or plastered. Sometimes known as a cradle roof. (27) SADDLEBACK: a tower roof where the top takes the form of an ordinary roof gable. (16)
Parts of a roof include: WALL or SOLE PLATE: the lowest longitudinal member of a truss resting on the wall and parallel to the first purlin. (26) PURLIN: a longitudinal member parallel to the wall but laid, usually at one-third or two-thirds intervals up the slope of the roof. (24, 25, 26, 28, 29) RIDGE: a member laid longitudinally at the apex of a roof and against which the upper ends of the rafters pitch or meet. (26, 28, 29) COMMON RAFTER: a member sloping from the wall plate to the ridge. (24, 25, 26, 28, 29) PRINCIPAL RAFTER: the main rafter in the construction of a roof truss. The rafter marking the principal divisions or bays of the space spanned. (24, 25, 26, 28, 29) SPROCKET: a piece of wood fixed to the foot of the rafters and overhanging the wall to give an extra lift to the eaves. BRACES: inclined or diagonally placed members, usually employed as a means of stiffening. (24)

WIND BRACES: diagonal braces crossing the rafters to stiffen the roof longitudinally and used to prevent racking. (26) COLLAR BEAM: a lateral beam, or tie beam, crossing higher up the roof, usually joining the opposite principal rafters. (24, 26, 29) TIE BEAM: a beam spanning the space from wall plate to wall plate, i.e. the lowest member of the truss, to prevent the wall from spreading. (24, 25, 28) HAMMER BEAM: a massive beam projecting horizontally from the top of a wall, but not meeting its corresponding member on the opposite side. In a complex roof, hammer beams may be piled one upon the other. This beam supports an ARCHED BRACE having a collar at its apex. It is itself supported by a smaller arched brace attached to a WALL POST (28, 29) which rests upon a corbel, the lowest part of this type of truss. (29) KING POST: a roof truss consisting of a central vertical member joining the tie beam to the ridge beam. (25) QUEEN POST: two vertical members placed symmetrically on a tie beam, rising to the junction of collar beam, purlin and principal rafter. (24) STRUT: a sloping or upright member placed between the tie beam or hammer beam and the principal rafter to give additional support to the rafter. (25, 28, 29) ASHLAR PIECES: short upright timbers fixed between the inner wall plate and the rafters. (26, 29)

ROPE MOULDING *see* CABLE MOULDING

ROSETTE. A circular ornament, carved, painted or moulded, resembling a formalised rose. (193) *See also* Patera

ROSE WINDOW. A circular window with concentric or radiating tracery patterns. Sometimes called a wheel window. (64)

ROSTRAL COLUMN *see* COLUMNA ROSTRATA

ROTUNDA. A building or internal space, circular or oval in plan and often domed. (145)

ROUNDEL. A circular panel, disc or medallion. Also a similarly shaped panel in a stained glass window. (200)

RUBBLE MASONRY. Walls made with rough uncut stones. COURSED RUBBLE: is built in regular layers or courses of a uniform height. (127) RANDOM RUBBLE: is built without courses. (214) SNECKED RUBBLE: in which the stones vary in size and the spaces left are filled with snecks or small rectangular fillings.

RUNNING DOG *see* VITRUVIAN SCROLL

RUSTICATION. A mode of building masonry, in which the individual blocks or courses of stone are emphasised by deeply recessed joints, and often by a roughened surface. BANDED: when only the horizontal joints are emphasised. (138) CHAMFERED: when the stones are smooth and separated by V-joints. (151) FROSTED: when the surface of the stones simulates icicles. (171) ROCK FACED: when the stones are given an irregular surface, to appear unhewn or weathered. (172) VERMICULATED: when the face of the stone gives the appearance of being worm-eaten. (136, 177)

SACRISTY. A room in, or attached to, a church, where are kept the sacred vessels. *See also* Vestry

SADDLEBACK ROOF *see* ROOF

SADDLE BAR. An iron bar fixed horizontally across a mullioned window to stiffen the leaded glazing. (55)

SANCTUARY. The holiest part of a church, around the high altar. The west–east sequence (in collegiate churches, cathedrals, etc.) of choir, presbytery and sanctuary is not, however, always clearly defined. (1, 6) *See also* Chancel, Choir, Presbytery

SANCTUS BELL-COTE *see* BELL-COTE

SASH. A glazed wooden frame, made so as to slide up and down by means of pulleys. A sash window is a double hung vertically sliding sash. (134, 182) *See also* Casement

SAXON *see* ANGLO-SAXON

SCAGLIOLA. A composition of sand, lime, gypsum and crushed stone polished to resemble marble

SCALLOPED CAPITAL. A type of cushion or block capital, in which the four sides are shaped into a series of curves or scallops. (44)

SCARP. A steep slope created in a fortification. (111)

SCOTIA. A small concave moulding between the two tori in the base of a column. It throws a deep shadow. (118, 119, 120, 121)

SCREEN. A partition of wood, metal or stone with one or more doors, enclosing part of a room or building. (190) Also a wall connecting two blocks of buildings or built out in front of a building and masking the façade, often in the form of a colonnade. (136) *See also* Parclose, Rood screen

SCREENS PASSAGE. The entrance passage separating the screen of a medieval hall from the kitchen, buttery and pantry. (184)

SCROLL MOULDING *see* ROLL MOULDING

SCROLLED PEDIMENT *see* PEDIMENT

SEDILIA. A series of seats (usually three), on the south side of the chancel, for the use of the clergy. Often recessed into the wall at three different levels, and crowned with carved canopies and pinnacles. (86)

SEGMENTAL ARCH *see* ARCH

SEGMENTAL PEDIMENT *see* PEDIMENT

SEMICIRCULAR ARCH *see* ARCH

SERLIANA or SERLIAN MOTIF *see* VENETIAN WINDOW

SETBACK BUTTRESS *see* BUTTRESS

SEVERY *see* VAULT

SEXPARTITE VAULT *see* VAULT

SHAFT. The body of a column between the base and capital. (117, 118, 119, 120, 121, 122) In medieval architecture the term is also applied to a small column, e.g. in a clustered pier supporting a vaulting rib. (68, 116)

SHAFT RING. A moulded ring around a circular pier or shaft attached to a pier. Sometimes called an annulet and seemingly indistinguishable from cincture.

SHAPED GABLE *see* GABLE

SHELL KEEP *see* KEEP

SHINGLES. Thin rectangular pieces of wood, with one end thicker than the other, used as roofing tiles. (17)

SHOULDERED ARCH *see* ARCH

SHOULDERED ARCHITRAVE *see* ARCHITRAVE

SILL, CILL. The horizontal base of a door or window frame. The threshold of a door. (183, 219)

SINGING GALLERY *see* ROOD LOFT

SINGLE-FRAMED ROOF *see* ROOF

SKEWBACK. Bevelled supporting stone at either end of a segmental or flat arch. (136)

SKIRTING. A narrow horizontal member, generally of wood, fixed to the bottom of an internal wall where it meets the floor. (200)

SKIRTING BLOCK *see* PLINTH BLOCK

SLATE HANGING and TILE HANGING. The covering of walls by hung overlapping rows of slates or tiles attached to a timber, brick or stone substructure. Sometimes shaped tiles are used to produce a fishscale effect. (220, 221)

SNECKED RUBBLE *see* RUBBLE MASONRY

SOFFIT. The undersurface of any architectural feature, e.g. of an arch, lintel, cornice, balcony, window or door head, etc. (122, 123) *See also* Archivolt

SOLAR, SOLLAR. A parlour or private room in medieval and Tudor manor houses, usually at first floor level, and approached by a stair from the dais end of the hall. (184)

SOLE PLATE *see* ROOF

SOLOMONIC ORDER *see* SPIRAL COLUMN

SOPRAPORTE *see* OVERDOOR

SOUNDING BOARD *see* TESTER

SPAN. The horizontal distance between two supporting members, such as the abutments of an arch, the walls carrying a roof, etc.

SPANDREL. The triangular area contained by one side of an arch, by a horizontal line taken from its apex, and by a vertical drawn from its springing; or the surface between two adjacent arches and the horizontal moulding or string cornice above them; or the triangular surface between the outer string of a stair and the floor; also, the surface of a vault between two adjacent ribs. (36, 67)

SPEER *see* SPUR

SPIRAL STAIR *see* STAIR

SPIRAL COLUMN. A twisted column, sometimes known as Solomonic order.

SPIRE. A tall tapering structure in the form of an elongated pyramid or cone, erected on the top of a tower, turret, roof, etc. (17) BROACH SPIRE: an octagonal spire on a square tower. Each of the four vacant spaces at the joining of the octagon and square is filled by a half-pyramid, the apex of which is in the centre of one of the sides of the spire. (18) NEEDLE SPIRE: a slender needle-like spire raised on the centre of a tower roof, also known as a Hertfordshire spike. (19) CROWN STEEPLE: an openwork spire resembling a crown. (20) HELM ROOF: an unusual form of spire with gables on each of the four sides and a pyramidal spire. (15) *See also* Roof — saddleback

SPIRELET. A very small spire. (129) *See also* Flèche

SPLAY. The diagonal surface formed by the chamfering or cutting away of a wall; especially the jamb of a window, when the opening is widened from the window to the face of the wall, allowing more light to enter. (92) *See also* Reveal

SPRING, SPRINGER, SPRINGING, SPRINGING LINE, SPRINGING POINT. The point at which an arch rises from its support. (46)

SPROCKET *see* ROOF

SPUR. In some medieval houses, a fixed screen opposite the entrance providing a draught-free sitting area around a fireplace. Also called a speer. (186) A grotesque, tongue or spray of foliage which fills the gap when a circular base of a column stands on a square or octagonal plinth. Found in early Gothic architecture. (101) A shore, prop or sloping buttress may also be termed a spur. (113)

SPUR STONE. A cylindrical stone fixed at the corner of a building on a street, to prevent damage to the angle from traffic. (224)

SQUARE. A quadrilateral area surrounded by buildings. Covent Garden (1630s) was the first square in London.

SQUINCH, SQUINCH ARCH. A small arch or series of concentric arches built across the angle of a square or polygon to support a superstructure, such as a spire or dome.

SQUINT. A small opening, cut through a wall, pier or partition of a church, to allow a view of the main altar from the aisles or side chapels. Also called a hagioscope. (75)

STADDLE STONES. Short mushroom-shaped stone posts, which support a stack or granary. Because of their shape, rats cannot climb up them. Now often used as garden ornaments. (223)

STAIR. A series or flight of steps, leading from one level to another; a staircase. DOGLEGGED STAIR: one without a central well and in which the flights are parallel, the handrail and strings running into the same newel. Introduced in the seventeenth century. (204) GEOMETRICAL STAIR: in which each stone step is built into the wall and rests on the step below. Usually on a round or elliptical plan. (206, 207) OPEN WELL or OPEN NEWEL STAIR: one which rises around a rectangular wall. (208) SPIRAL STAIR or NEWEL STAIR: also known as a VICE STAIR or WINDING

STAIR: circular stair with tapered steps which wind around a central pillar or newel. (205)

STALLS. Fixed seats usually arranged along the south and north walls of a choir or chancel, for the use of the clergy and choir. Often elaborately carved with misericords and provided with canopies. (94)

STANDING *see* BELVEDERE

STEEPLE. The complete tower of a church, with its spire, lantern, etc. (18)

STELLAR VAULT *see* VAULT

STIFF LEAF. Lobe-shaped sculptured foliage found on Early English capitals. (71)

STILE. The end vertical member of a door or window frame, or in panelling, the vertical member into which the horizontal rails are fixed. (187) *See also* Muntin, Rail

STILTED ARCH *see* ARCH

STILTED VAULT *see* VAULT

STOP *see* CHAMFER

STOPPED CHAMFER *see* CHAMFER

STOUP. A vessel to contain holy water, sometimes freestanding, but usually fixed to, or carved out of, a wall. Placed near the door of a church. (88)

STRAINER ARCH. An arch spanning a space between two verticals to transfer pressure or to prevent the bulging of a wall. (79)

STRAPWORK. A form of sixteenth-century decoration consisting of interlacing bands, resembling straps, sometimes combined with other grotesque forms on ceilings, pilasters, panels, etc. (190)

STRETCHER *see* BRICKWORK

STRIGES *see* FLUTES, FLUTING

STRING. One of the two sloping members carrying the ends of the treads and risers of a staircase. The one attached to the wall is the WALL STRING, the other supported by the newels is the OUTER STRING. An OPEN STRING or CUT STRING is an outer string which is cut to the profile of the steps. (209, 210, 211)

STRING COURSE. A moulding or projecting band running horizontally across a façade. (134)

STRUT *see* ROOF

STUDS. Intermediate vertical posts in a timber-framed partition or wall. (164, 168) When set at a little more than its own width apart, and infilled with plaster, called close studding.

STYLOBATE. A continuous base to a colonnade, such as the step or steps on which the colonnade is placed. (140, 163)

SUMMER. A main beam in a structure, especially the main beam supporting the joists of a floor. (45) *See also* Bressumer

SUNK CHAMFER *see* CHAMFER

SURBASE. The crowning moulding of a base, pedestal, podium, etc., above the dado. (201)

SWAG. A festoon in which the object suspended resembles a piece of cloth. (177, 191) *See also* Festoon

SWELLED FRIEZE *see* PULVINATED FRIEZE

SYSTYLE *see* INTERCOLUMNIATION

TABERNACLE. An ornamental niche or receptacle above an altar which contains the Holy Sacrament. A temporary place of worship, especially the temporary churches built in London after the Great Fire of 1666.

TABERNACLE WORK. The elaborate carved work on canopies over niches, stalls, pulpits and on church screens. (94)

TELAMONES *see* ATLANTES

TEMPLATE. The block of stone on top of a wall to carry the weight of a joist or roof truss. Sometimes called templet.

TEMPLE. A building for religious worship. In England, columnar classical models were frequently adopted for garden buildings dedicated to the Virtues, Elements, etc. The term is also loosely applied in this country to garden buildings in the Chinese, Gothic, Moorish and other non-classical styles. The classical forms are classified according to (i) the order of columns used, e.g. Doric, Ionic, Corinthian. (ii) The disposition of the columns; PROSTYLE: with a portico in front; (140) AMPHIPROSTYLE: with front and rear porticos; PERIPTERAL: with two porticos and side colonnades, surrounding the building with a single range of columns (the range of columns and the space between the wall of the buildings and the columns is called the peristyle); PSEUDOPERIPTERAL: with two porticos and engaged columns or pilasters on the sides; DIPTERAL: when surrounded by two ranges of columns; PSEUDODIPTERAL: is similar to the dipteral, but has the inner range of columns omitted. (iii) The number of columns in the portico, e.g. DISTYLE (two), TETRASTYLE (three), (141) HEXASTYLE (six), OCTASTYLE (eight), DECASTYLE (ten), DODECASTYLE (twelve). A cella is that part of a temple, exclusive of the portico.

TEMPLET *see* TEMPLATE

TENIA. The uppermost fillet on a Doric architrave, separating it from the frieze. (118)

TERM, TERMINAL FIGURE, HERM. A pedestal, pier, pilaster, etc., tapering towards the base and having a sculptured head or upper part of a human figure growing out of it. Often used in gardens to define boundaries. (146)

TERRACE. A level promenade usually in front of a building and confined by a balustrade. The term also refers to a continuous and more or less uniform row of houses. (160)

TESSELLATED PAVEMENT. A decorative floor or wall mosaic made up of small blocks of stone, marble, tile, earthenware, etc., called tesserae, embedded in cement. (44)

TESTER. A flat canopy serving as a sounding board over a pulpit. Also the canopy over a bed, throne, etc. (92)

TETRASTYLE *see* TEMPLE

THATCH. Straw, reed, heather, etc. used as a roof covering. (156, 217)

THERM WINDOW *see* DIOCLETIAN WINDOW

THREE-CENTRED ARCH *see* ARCH

THROAT, THROATING. A groove or channel on the underside of a projecting sill, coping, etc., forming a drip to prevent water from running back to dampen the wall face. *See also* Drip

TIE BEAM *see* ROOF

TIERCERONS *see* VAULT

TILE HANGING *see* SLATE HANGING and TILE
HANGING

TIMBER FRAMING. A form of building in which walls and partitions
are built as a timber framework and filled in with plaster, brickwork, stone,
wattle and daub, etc. Sometimes the timber is covered with weather-boarding
or tiling. Used from the fifteenth to the eighteenth century. Also called half-
timber construction. (168)

TORUS. A bold convex moulding used in the bases of columns. (117, 118,
119, 120, 121)

TOWER. A tall building, either isolated or forming part of a church, castle,
etc. (2, 8, 18, 107, 126, 138)

TRABEATED. A building constructed on the post-and-lintel method, in
contrast to an arcuated one.

TRACERY. The ornamental work formed by the branching of mullions in
the upper part of a Gothic window. PLATE TRACERY: the earliest and most
elementary form of tracery, having the effect of simple, round openings cut
out of a stone in-filling or plate. (53) BAR TRACERY: a development of plate
tracery *c.* 1245 using slender shafts and shaped members branching out from
the mullions to form a decorative pattern in the window head. GEOMETRICAL
TRACERY: consisting of simple symmetrical shapes, such as circles, trefoils,
etc. (54) Y-TRACERY: where a mullion splits to form a Y shape. (55) INTER-
SECTED TRACERY: a development and amplification of Y-tracery, in which
each mullion branches out into two curved bars intersecting the adjacent
bars; thus each group of two or three lights can be regarded as an arch within
arch. (56) FLOWING TRACERY or CURVILINEAR TRACERY: a fourteenth-
century form, sometimes in conjunction with geometrical tracery, consisting
of sinuous lines with circles drawn at top and bottom into ogee shapes. (57)
Where these shapes occur in rows, RETICULATED TRACERY results. (58)

In KENTISH TRACERY, so called because it occurs mostly in Kent, a split cusp is used. (59) FLAMBOYANT TRACERY: essentially a French form of tracery but found occasionally in this country. It is a further development of flowing tracery, but has an upward tendency, giving a flame-like form. (60) RECTILINEAR, PANEL or PERPENDICULAR TRACERY: was introduced in the fifteenth century. The mullions now pass uninterrupted to the head of the arch. The tracery consists of upright, straight-sided panels above the window lights. (61) DROP TRACERY: a pendant tracery border on the intrados of an arch. (65) *See also* Cusp, Dagger, Foil, Mouchette

TRANSEPT. The transverse arm of a cruciform church. (1, 4)

TRANSITIONAL. Between any two consecutive architectural styles, there is always an in-between stage, when features from the two styles are combined. The term Transitional usually refers to the period between Norman and Early English, when for example, capitals with carved leaf foliage may be found under semi-circular arches. (68)

TRANSOM. A horizontal member dividing a window. (137, 169) *See also* Mullion

TRANSVERSE RIB *see* VAULT

TREAD. In a staircase, the horizontal part of a step. (209, 210, 211) *See also* Riser

TREFOIL *see* FOIL

TREFOIL ARCH *see* ARCH

TRIBUNE *see* GALLERY

TRIFORIUM. The wall passage (or blank arcading) open to the nave by arches, above the nave arcades (i.e. above the aisles), below the aisle roofs, and, from the nave elevation, below the clerestory. (66)

TRIGLYPH. One of the rectangular blocks between the metopes in a

Doric frieze, having two vertical grooves or glyphs in the centre and half-grooves on the edges, hence three grooves or triglyphs. (118)

TROPHY. A sculptured group of arms and armour. Usually an emblem of battle or memorial of battles won. (176)

TRUMEAU. A vertical stone member or mullion supporting the tympanum of a doorway. A useful term borrowed from the French. (46, 91)

TRUSS *see* CONSOLE

TRUSS *see* ROOF

TUDOR. The period (1485–1603) and style extending from the late Perpendicular to the end of Queen Elizabeth's reign. Brick is a characteristic material. (165, 168)

TUDOR FLOWER. An upright diamond-shaped or three lobed leaf-like ornament used in Tudor decoration. (81) *See also* Brattishing

TUNNEL VAULT *see* VAULT

TURRET. A small tower of round or polygonal plan. Often containing a newel stair. (107)

TUSCAN BASE *see* BASE

TUSCAN ORDER *see* ORDER

TYMPANUM. The triangular or segmental space between the enclosing mouldings of a pediment. (141) In medieval architecture, the space between the lintel of a doorway and the arch above it. (46)

U NDERCROFT. A vaulted underground room. (85) *See also* Crypt

V ALLEY. The internal angle formed by the intersection of the sloping sides of a roof. (127)

VANE. A thin plate of metal, often ornamental in form, mounted upon a vertical spindle, so as to turn with the wind. (8) *See also* Weathervane

VAULT. An arched roof or ceiling; (3) also an underground chamber for burial or storage. BARREL VAULT: an uninterrupted vault of semicircular section, also called a TUNNEL VAULT or WAGONHEAD VAULT. (30) GROINED VAULT or CROSS VAULT: a type of vaulting which takes its name from the arched diagonals or groins formed by the intersection of two barrel vaults at right angles. (31) DOMICAL VAULT: a groined vault, in which the groins are semicircular, rather than semi-elliptical as in a simple groined vault. As a result, the centre of the vaulted bay rises higher than its outer arches and is curved like a dome. (41) RIB or RIBBED VAULT: a system of cross vaulting in which the groins are replaced by arched ribs constructed across the sides and diagonals of the vaulted bay to act as a framework or support for the infilling or web. (32) QUADRIPARTITE VAULT: a rib vault in which each bay is divided by two diagonal ribs into four compartments. (33) SEXPARTITE VAULT: where each bay is divided into six parts by two diagonal ribs and one transverse rib. (34) PLOUGHSHARE or STILTED VAULT: a vault in which the wall ribs, in order to increase the light from a clerestory window, are sprung from a higher level than the diagonal ribs, thus producing a warped, twisting surface or web, resembling a ploughshare. (35) LIERNE VAULT: a ribbed vault to which secondary ribs or liernes, which do not spring from the wall supports, are added to link the main ribs and tiercerons. (38) STELLAR VAULT: a vault in which the main ribs, ridge rib, tiercerons and liernes are so arranged as to produce a star-shaped pattern. (37) FAN VAULT: a vault composed of inverted concave cones overlaid with numerous ribs of the same curve and length, radiating at equal angles from one springer and thus producing a fan-like pattern. (39, 40) RIBS: the projecting bands of stone or brick which support or decorate a vault. DIAGONAL RIBS: the pair of arched ribs thrown diagonally across a square or rectangular bay, from springer to springer, to support a vault. (32, 36) The point at which they intersect is called the CROWN and is often

Vault

ornamented with a BOSS. (36) WALL RIBS or FORMERETS: the half ribs arched across the lateral wall space of a vaulted bay to complete the design, but not for any structural purpose. (32) TRANSVERSE RIB: the rib running at right angles to a wall across the width of the space that is vaulted. They support the vault and define the bays. (32, 36) RIDGE RIB: a secondary decorative or structural rib placed along the longitudinal or transverse axis of a vault. (32, 36) TIERCERONS or INTERMEDIATE RIBS: issuing from the main springers and inserted between the transverse and diagonal ribs to give additional support. They generally butt on to the ridge rib. (36) LIERNE RIBS: secondary ribs which do not originate either from the main springers or the central boss, and are employed as decorative links between the main ribs and tiercerons. (38) WEB: the stone infilling or surface between the ribs, sometimes called a cell. (32) SEVERY: a bay or compartment of a vault. (32) VAULT or VAULTING SHAFT: the vertical shaft from which the vault ribs spring. (33) GROIN: the sharp edge or arris, made by the junction of two vaulting surfaces. (31)

VENETIAN DOOR. The form of a Venetian window applied to a door, i.e. having sidelights on each side of its frame. (174)

VENETIAN WINDOW. A tripartite window, the central opening being arched and wider than the side openings, which have flat heads. Also called a Palladian window, or Serliana or Serlian Motif because it was first illustrated in Serlio's *Architettura*, 1537. (136)

VERANDA, VERANDAH. An open gallery with a roof on light, usually metal supports, placed along the front (and occasionally other sides) of a building. (161)

VERGE BOARDS *see* BARGE BOARDS

VERMICULATED *see* RUSTICATION

VERMICULATION *see* RUSTICATION

VERNACULAR STYLE. A native or local style, usually conservative in comparison to that of metropolitan centres. Classical forms are generally absent. A style particularly associated with cottages and small houses, and often conditioned by the use of local building materials. Vernacular building is folk building to be distinguished from guild building. (164)

VESICA PISCIS (a fish's bladder). A pointed oval shape. When framing the figure of Christ called a mandorla or aureole. (84)

VESTRY. A room in or attached to a church, where vestments are kept and where the clergy and choir robe. *See also* Sacristy

VICE, VISE, VYS *see* STAIR

VILLA. In the early eighteenth century the term was derived from Palladio's *case di villa* meaning a country estate. The term was later applied to a compact house (of five bays 1-3-1), sometimes a secondary seat of a nobleman, and usually in a suburban (i.e. Thames Valley) situation. With the advent of the Picturesque, Villa could mean not only a type related to the Italian vernacular (e.g. Nash's Cronkhill) but one that gradually became synonymous with an abode of the middle classes, adhering to no specific architectural formula. (159)

VITRUVIAN OPENING. A doorway or window in which the width between the jambs narrows to the top, as advocated by Vitruvius and Palladio. (163)

VITRUVIAN SCROLL. A running spiral pattern rather like a series of waves. Also called a wave scroll and sometimes a running dog. (195)

VOLUTE. A spiral scroll, the distinctive feature of the Ionic capital and also used in modified form in Corinthian and Composite capitals, and in consoles and brackets. (119, 121, 195)

VOUSSOIR. One of a series of wedge-shaped stones or bricks used to form an arch. (136, 147)

Wagonhead Vault *see* VAULT

WAGON ROOF *see* ROOF

WAINSCOT. A term used for wood panelling generally and also to describe panelling which goes up to dado height only. (187)

WALL ARCADE *see* BLIND ARCADE

WALL PLATE *see* ROOF

WALL RIBS *see* VAULT

WALL POST *see* ROOF

WALL STRING *see* STRING

WARD *see* BAILEY

WATER LEAF. A motif used in later twelfth-century capitals, based on a water-lily or lotus leaf. The tapered end curves up towards the angle of the abacus and turns in at the top. (69)

WATER TABLE *see* WEATHERING

WATTLE AND DAUB. A primitive infilling between the members of a timber-framed wall, formed of split staves or laths roughly plastered with clay. (215)

WAVE SCROLL *see* VITRUVIAN SCROLL

WEATHER BOARDING. Overlapping horizontal boards fixed on the external wall of timber-framed buildings. Most common in East Anglia and southern England. (167) *See also* Slate hanging and Tile hanging

WEATHERING. An inclined surface on top of a projection such as a cornice, sill or the offsets of a buttress, to throw off rainwater. Sometimes called a water table or off-set. (83)

WEATHERVANE. A vane usually combined with crossed rods to show the four compass points, to indicate the direction of the wind. Sometimes shaped like a cock, hence weathercock. (18, 19)

WEB *see* VAULT

WELL, WELL HOLE. The open vertical space or hole between the outer stringers of an open stair which has two or more flights.

WHEEL WINDOW *see* ROSE WINDOW

WIND BRACES *see* ROOF

WINDER. A step in a winding stair, which is narrower at one end than the other. (92)

WINDING STAIR *see* STAIR

Y-TRACERY *see* TRACERY

ZIG-ZAG *see* CHEVRON

—

BIBLIOGRAPHY

Bibliography of books consulted in the preparation of the Glossary.

Architectural Publications Society. *The Dictionary of Architecture* (ed. Wyatt Papworth), 11 vols, 1852–.

Atkinson, T. D., *A Glossary of Terms used in English Architecture*, 1906.

Barley, M. W., *The English Farmhouse and Cottage*, 1961.

Betjeman, J., *Collins Guide to English Parish Churches*, 1958.

Bond, F., *Gothic Architecture in England*, 1906.

Braun, H., *Historical Architecture*, 1962.

Briggs, M. S., *Everyman's Concise Encyclopaedia of Architecture*, 1959.

Britton, J., *A Dictionary of the Architecture and Archaeology of the Middle Ages*, 2 vols, 1838.

Clifton-Taylor, A., *The Pattern of English Building*, 1962.

Crossley, F. H., *Timber Buildings in England*, 1951.

Dollman, F. T. and Jobbins, I. R., *An Analysis of Ancient Domestic Architecture in Great Britain*, vol. II, 1863.

Fletcher, Sir Banister, *A History of Architecture on the Comparative Method*, 17th ed., 1961.

Gwilt, J., *An Encyclopaedia of Architecture* (ed. Wyatt Papworth), 1912.

Gwilt, J., *A Treatise on the Decorative Part of Civil Architecture by Sir William Chambers*, 1862.

Harvey, J., *English Cathedrals*, 1956.

Hughes, Q. and Lynton, N., *Simpson's History of Architectural Development*, vol. IV, Renaissance Architecture, 1962.

Lloyd, Nathaniel, *A History of the English House*, 1931.

Murray, P. and L., *A Dictionary of Art and Artists*, 1959.

Bibliography

Nicholson, P., *An Architectural Dictionary*, 2 vols, 1819.

Osborne, A. L., *A Dictionary of English Domestic Architecture*, 1954.

Parker, J. H., *A Glossary of Terms used in Grecian, Roman, Italian and Gothic Architecture*, 1850.

Pevsner, N., *The Buildings of England*, series — continuing.

Plommer, H., *Simpson's History of Architectural Development*, vol. I, Ancient and Classical Architecture, 1956.

Robertson, D. S., *A Handbook of Greek and Roman Architecture*, 1945.

Royal Commission on Historical Monuments, England, series — continuing.

The Shorter Oxford English Dictionary, 1944.

Smith, J. T., 'Medieval Roofs: a Classification', in *The Archaeological Journal*, vol. CXV, 1958.

A Society of Architects, *The Builder's Magazine*, 1774.

Statham, H. H., *A History of Architecture*, 1950.

Stewart, C., *Simpson's History of Architectural Development*, vol. II, Early Christian Byzantine and Romanesque Architecture, 1954.

Stewart, C., *Simpson's History of Architectural Development*, vol. III, Gothic Architecture, 1961.

Stuart, R., *A Dictionary of Architecture*, 3 vols, 182–.

Summerson, Sir John, *The Classical Language of Architecture*, 1963.

Ware, D. and Beatty, B., *A Short Dictionary of Architecture*, 1953.

Webb, G., *Architecture in Britain. The Middle Ages*, 1956.

PLATES

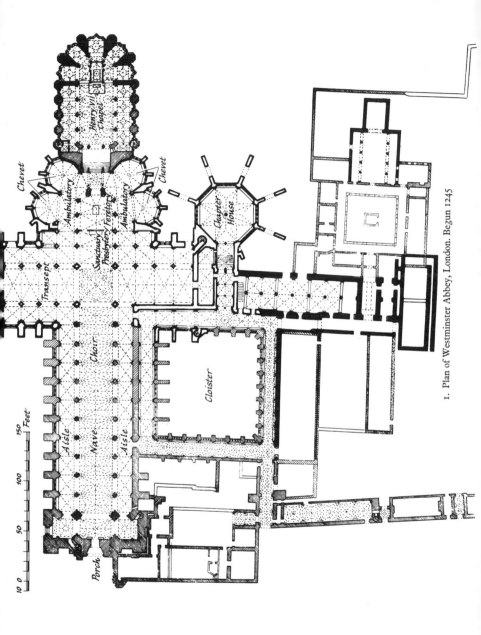

1. Plan of Westminster Abbey, London. Begun 1245

TOWER

NAVE

PORCH

2. West front, Westminster Abbey. 14th and 15th century,
the towers designed by Nicholas Hawksmoor, 1735–40

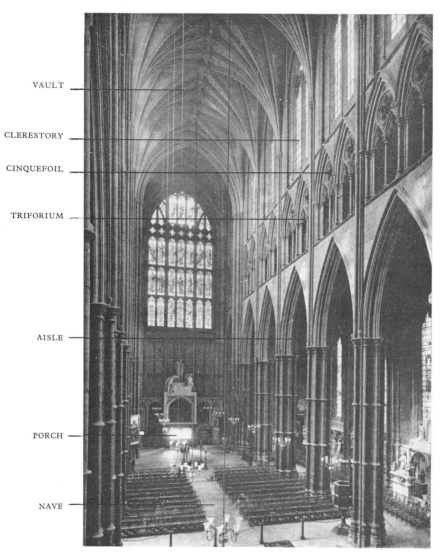

VAULT

CLERESTORY

CINQUEFOIL

TRIFORIUM

AISLE

PORCH

NAVE

3. Nave looking towards the west end, Westminster Abbey.
West end completed *c.* 1512

TRANSEPT

NAVE

AISLE

PORCH

4. View from north, Westminster Abbey, 13th century and later restorations

CHAPTER
HOUSE

CHEVET

5. Chapter House, Westminster Abbey. c. 1235–53

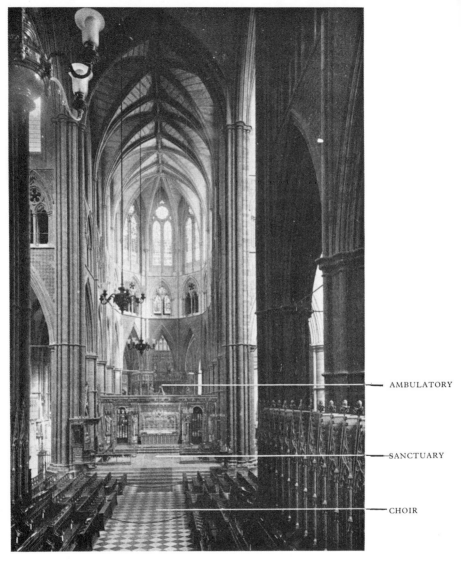

AMBULATORY

SANCTUARY

CHOIR

6. View into chancel, begun 1245. Westminster Abbey

CHEVET

SHAFT RING

AMBULATORY

7. Ambulatory, 13th century. Westminster Abbey

VANE

TOWER

NAVE

CASTELLATED

AISLE

CHANCEL

8. Chipping Campden, Gloucestershire. Perpendicular. View from south-east

CHANCEL

AISLE

NAVE

9. Nave looking east. Chipping Campden, Gloucestershire

10. Clasping buttresses, Norman. Thockington Church, Northumberland

11. Diagonal buttresses, early 14th century. All Saints, Crostwight, Norfolk

12. Setback buttresses, 15th century. Campanile of Chichester Cathedral, Sussex

13. Angle buttresses, Perpendicular. St Andrew, Deopham, Norfolk

14. Flying buttresses, 14th century. Westminster Abbey, London

15. Anglo-Saxon helm roof, 11th century. St Mary, Sompting, Sussex

BELFRY

LOUVER

CREST TILE

16. Double saddleback roof, 18th or 19th century.
St Bartholomew, Fingest, Buckinghamshire

SHINGLES

17. Timber spire, late 13th century style. All Saints, Monkland, Herefordshire

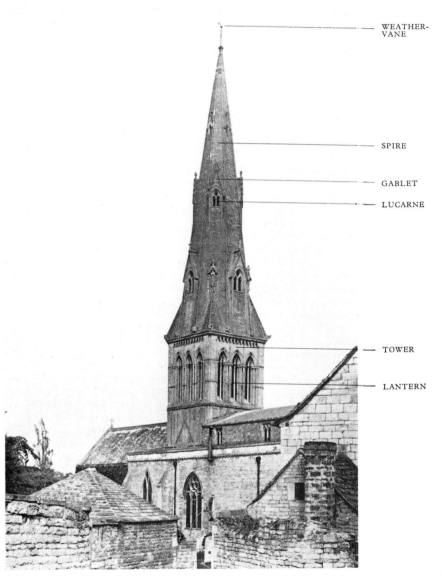

WEATHER-
VANE

SPIRE

GABLET

LUCARNE

TOWER

LANTERN

18. Broach spire, 14th century. St Mary the Virgin, Ketton, Rutland

WEATHER-
VANE

LOOP HOLE

19. Needle spire, 14th century. St Mary, Ashwell, Hertfordshire

FINIAL

PINNACLE

20. Crown steeple, 18th century. St Mary, Faversham, Kent

FLÈCHE

CLERESTORY

PRIEST'S
DOOR

21. Flèche, St Edmund, Southwold, Suffolk

22. Lean-to roof. All Saints, Mattishall, Norfolk

23. Couple roof, 15th century. St Peter, Reymerston, Norfolk

PURLIN

BRACE

COLLAR
BEAM

QUEEN POST

COMMON
RAFTER

PRINCIPAL
RAFTER

TIE BEAM

24. Queen post roof, Early Tudor. St Giles, Holme, Nottinghamshire

PURLIN

COMMON
RAFTER

PURLIN

STRUT

KING POST

TIE BEAM

PRINCIPAL
RAFTER

25. King post roof, All Saints, Markham Clinton, Nottinghamshire

COMMON RAFTER
PRINCIPAL RAFTER
COLLAR BEAM
ARCHED BRACE
RIDGE
WALL PLATE
CORBEL
ASHLAR PIECES
PURLIN
ARCHED WIND BRACES

26. Braced collar roof, 15th century. Hall of Vicars, Wells, Somerset

27. Wagon roof, 14th century. St Andrew, Tarvin, Cheshire

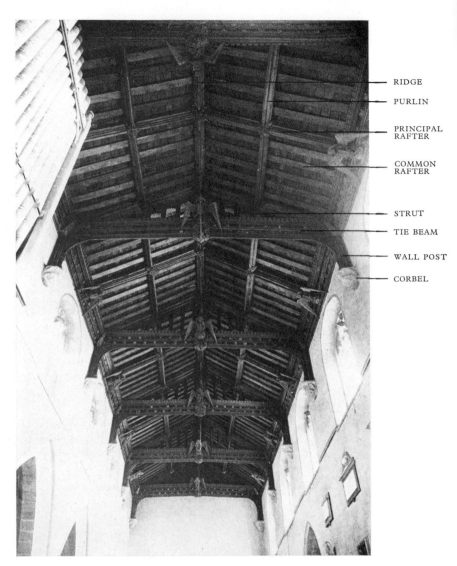

RIDGE

PURLIN

PRINCIPAL
RAFTER

COMMON
RAFTER

STRUT

TIE BEAM

WALL POST

CORBEL

28. Nave roof, 15th century. St John Baptist, Pilton, Somerset

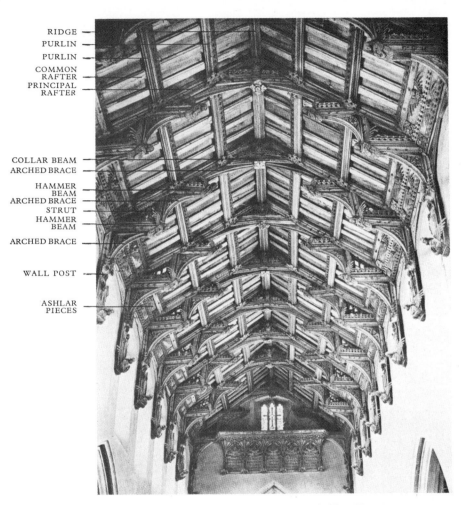

RIDGE
PURLIN
PURLIN
COMMON
RAFTER
PRINCIPAL
RAFTER

COLLAR BEAM
ARCHED BRACE

HAMMER
BEAM
ARCHED BRACE
STRUT
HAMMER
BEAM

ARCHED BRACE

WALL POST

ASHLAR
PIECES

29. Double hammer beam roof, 15th century. St Mary, Woolpit, Suffolk

30. Barrel vault, 11th century. Dark Cloister, Westminster Abbey, London

ARCHIVOLT

GROIN

CUSHION
CAPITAL

ABUTMENT

31. Groined vault, Norman. Crypt. Canterbury Cathedral, Kent

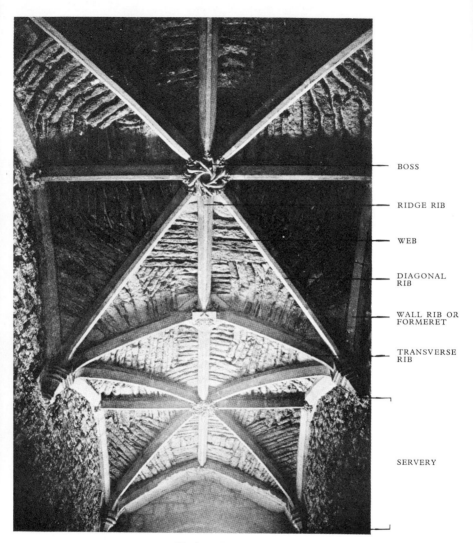

BOSS

RIDGE RIB

WEB

DIAGONAL
RIB

WALL RIB OR
FORMERET

TRANSVERSE
RIB

SERVERY

32. Vaulting, 15th century. Westbury College, Bristol, Somerset

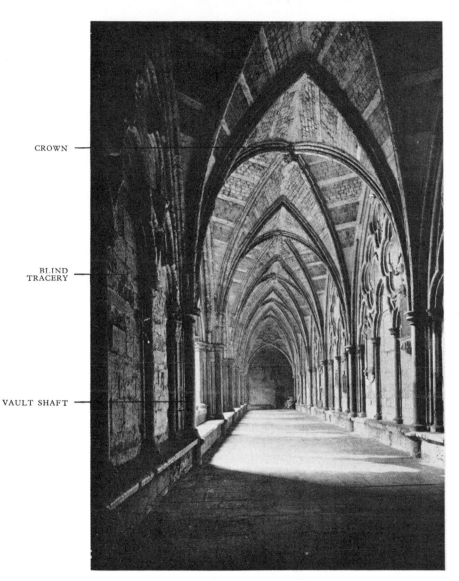

CROWN

BLIND
TRACERY

VAULT SHAFT

33. Quadripartite vaulting, 13th century. North walk of
cloisters, Westminster Abbey, London

34. Sexpartite vaulting, 13th century. South-east transept, Lincoln Cathedral

35. Ploughshare vault, 13th century. Chancel, Southwark Cathedral, London

BOSS

RIDGE RIB

TIERCERON

DIAGONAL RIB

TIERCERON

TRANSVERSE RIB

SPANDREL

36. Nave vault, mid 13th century. Lincoln Cathedral

37. Stellar vault, 14th century. Lady Chapel, Wells Cathedral, Somerset

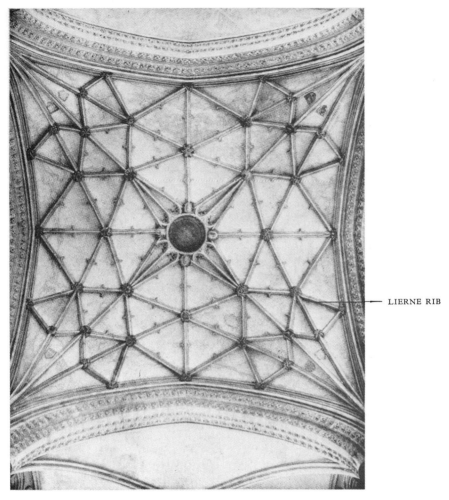

LIERNE RIB

38. Lierne vault, 15th century. Crossing, Salisbury Cathedral, Wiltshire

BLIND
TRACERY

39. Fan vault, late 14th century. Cloisters, Gloucester Cathedral

PENDANT

DROP
TRACERY

40. Fan vault with pendants, 16th century. Henry VII Chapel, Westminster Abbey, London

41. Domical vault in a hall church. Christ Church, Bristol, Somerset. 1786–90

BEAKHEAD

JAMB

42. Semi-circular Norman arch. St Peter, Windrush, Gloucestershire

DOGTOOTH

IMPOST

43. Round trefoil Norman arch. St Mary, Clymping, Sussex

BILLET

SCALLOPED
CAPITAL

PILLAR

TESSELLATED
PAVEMENT

44. Stilted Norman arch. St Bartholomew the Great, Smithfield, London

JOIST

SUMMER

45. Shouldered Norman arch. Boothby Pagnell Manor House, Lincolnshire

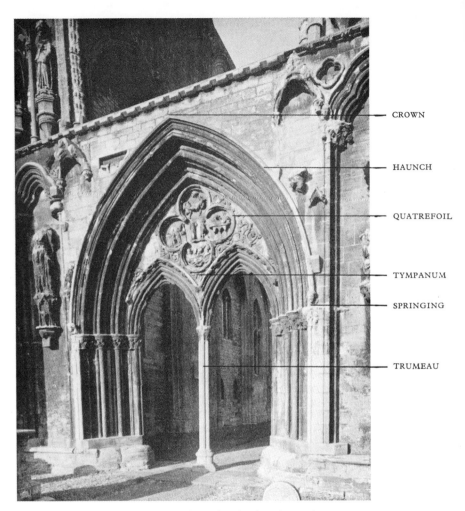

CROWN

HAUNCH

QUATREFOIL

TYMPANUM

SPRINGING

TRUMEAU

46. West door of ruined nave, late 12th and early 15th centuries.
Crowland Abbey, Lincolnshire

DIAPER ——

47. Ogee Decorated arch. Choir screen, Lincoln Cathedral

HOOD MOULD

LABEL STOP

MOULDED
CHAMFER

48. Three-centred arch, 15th century. Door to porch staircase,
St Mary, Attleborough, Norfolk

GALLETING

49. Four-centred arch. The Castle, Walmer, Kent. 1539

50. Segmental arch and Greek Doric columns. Carlton House Terrace, London. John Nash, 1827–9

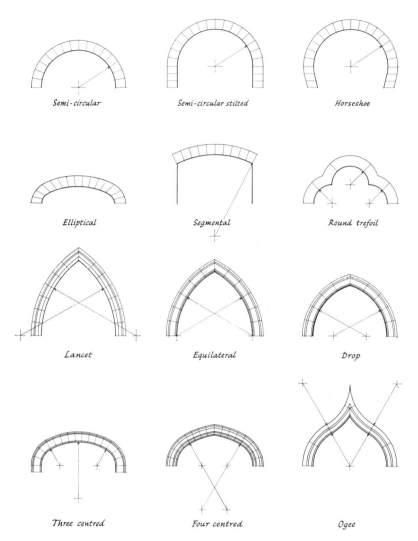

Semi-circular

Semi-circular stilted

Horseshoe

Elliptical

Segmental

Round trefoil

Lancet

Equilateral

Drop

Three centred

Four centred

Ogee

51. A selection of the principal forms of arches

52. Early English lancet windows. Holy Cross, Stoke Holy Cross, Norfolk

RAINWATER
HEAD

53. Plate tracery, 13th century. The Hall, Winchester Castle, Hampshire

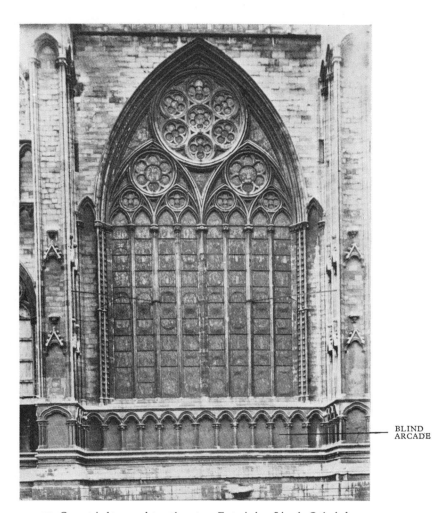

BLIND
ARCADE

54. Geometrical tracery, late 13th century. East window, Lincoln Cathedral

SADDLE BAR

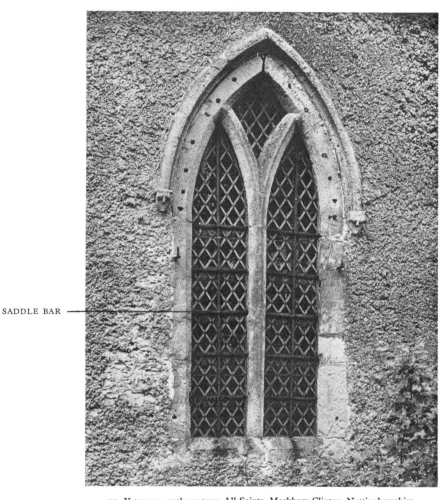

55. Y-tracery, 13th century. All Saints, Markham Clinton, Nottinghamshire

56. Intersected tracery, 13th century. East window, All Saints, Sharrington, Norfolk

CHEQUER
WORK

57. Flowing tracery, 14th century. South aisle, St Mary, Harefield, Middlesex

QUARRY

58. Reticulated tracery, 14th century. St James, West Hanney, Berkshire

59. Kentish tracery, 14th century. East window, St Mary, Chartham, Kent

60. Flamboyant tracery, late 14th century. Salford Priors, Warwickshire

EMBATTLED

MULLION

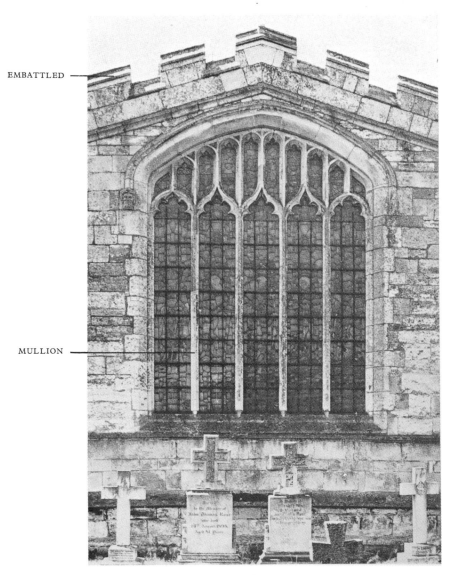

61. Panel tracery, late 14th century. East window, St John
Baptist, East Markham, Nottinghamshire

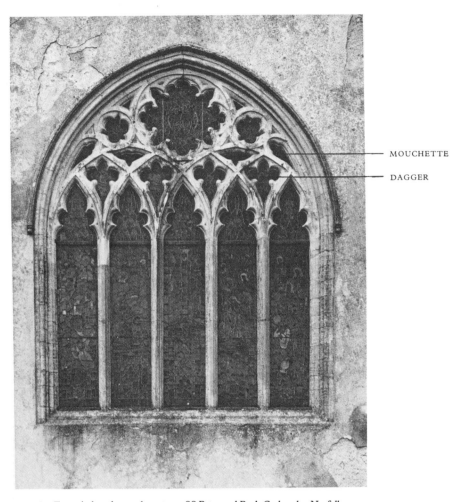

MOUCHETTE

DAGGER

62. East window, late 13th century. SS Peter and Paul, Carbrooke, Norfolk

MOUCHETTE ——————

FOIL ——————
CUSP ——————

63. 14th century window. St Mary, Amport, Hampshire

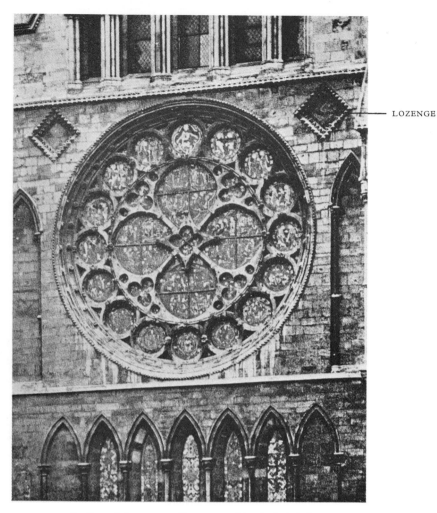

LOZENGE

64. Rose window, *c.* 1325. East transept, Lincoln Cathedral

DROP
TRACERY

65. Drop tracery, 14th century. North chancel chapel, St Peter, Maxey, Northamptonshire

CHEVRON

CUSHION CAPITAL

RESPOND

66. Norman triforium, Durham Cathedral

SPANDREL

ROLL AND
FILLET

67. Blind arcade, 13th century. North aisle, Lady Chapel, Worcester Cathedral

ARCHIVOLT

DOG TOOTH

QUIRK

HOLLOW
CHAMFER

SHAFT

68. Norman crocket capital. The Hall, Oakham Castle, Rutland

ARRIS

WATERLEAF

69. Water leaf capital, late 12th century. St John Baptist,
North Luffenham, Rutland

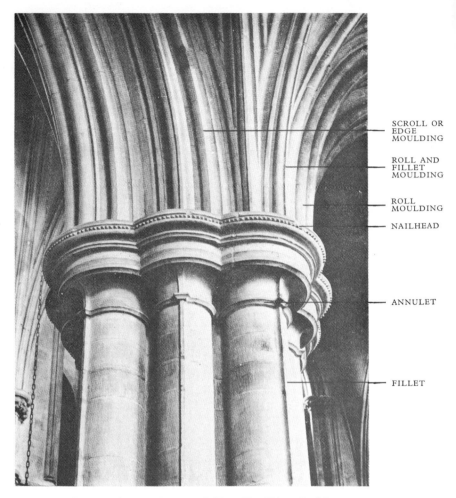

SCROLL OR
EDGE
MOULDING

ROLL AND
FILLET
MOULDING

ROLL
MOULDING

NAILHEAD

ANNULET

FILLET

70. Clustered column, 13th century. St Mary, West Walton, Norfolk

SCROLL OR
EDGE
MOULDING

ROLL
MOULDING

71. Stiff leaf capital, 13th century. St Mary, West Walton, Norfolk

LESENE

LONG AND
SHORT WORK

72. Late Saxon tower. All Saints, Earls Barton, Northamptonshire

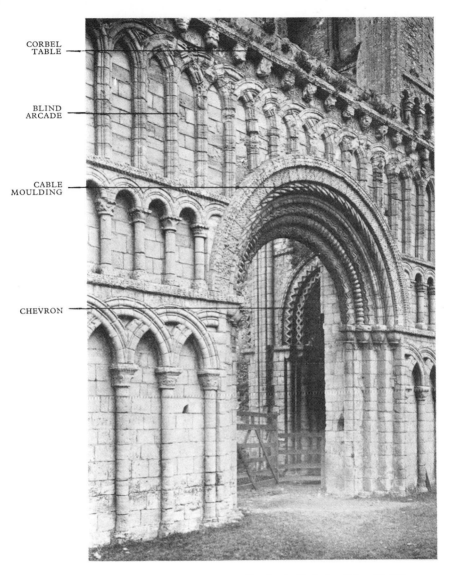

CORBEL
TABLE

BLIND
ARCADE

CABLE
MOULDING

CHEVRON

73. Norman blind arcading, West façade, Castle Acre Priory, Norfolk

ROOD STAIR

STOPPED
CHAMFER

74. Rood stair, St Lawrence the Martyr, Long Coombe, Oxfordshire

BOWTELL

SQUINT

CHANCEL

75. Chancel arch, 12th century. St Michael, Stoke Charity, Hampshire

76. Ceilure, 15th century. St Mary, Hennock, Devon

ROOD LOFT

ROOD SCREEN

77. Rood screen and loft. St James, Avebury, Wiltshire. 15th century, but restored 20th

CRESTING

78. Pulpitum, 14th century. Southwell Minster, Nottinghamshire

SUNK
CHAMFER

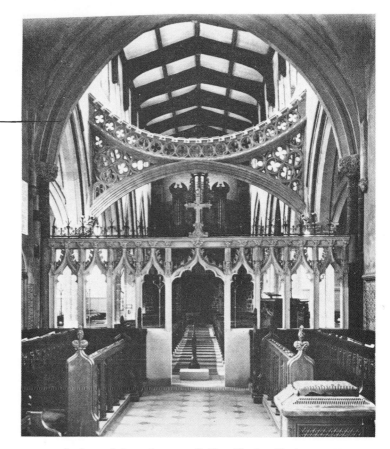

79. Strainer arch, late 14th century. St Mary, Finedon, Northamptonshire

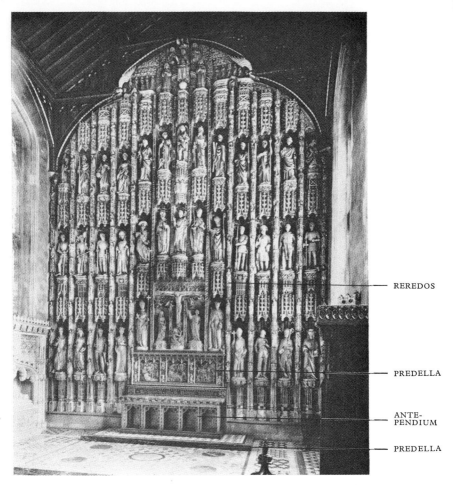

REREDOS

PREDELLA

ANTE-
PENDIUM

PREDELLA

80. Reredos, late 15th century, and altar, 19th century. All Souls College, Oxford

TUDOR
FLOWER

BRATTISHING

81. Parclose screen, 15th century. St John Baptist, East Markham, Nottinghamshire

82. Galilee, 13th century. Ely Cathedral, Cambridgeshire

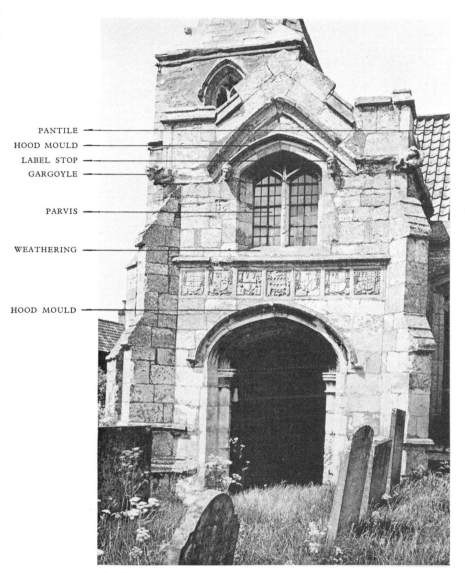

PANTILE

HOOD MOULD

LABEL STOP

GARGOYLE

PARVIS

WEATHERING

HOOD MOULD

83. Porch with 'parvis' above, late 15th century. St Giles, Holme, Nottinghamshire

VESICA
PISCIS

84. Vesica Piscis, Norman door. St Nicholas, Barfreston, Kent

85. Undercroft, 12th century. Fountains Abbey, Yorkshire

CROCKET

AUMBRY

86. Sedilia, 14th century. St Mary Magdalen, Helmdon, Northamptonshire

CABLE
MOULDING

87. Norman fcnt. St Andrew, Windsor, Berkshire

88. Stoup, St Mary Swanton, Swardeston, Norfolk

BALL
FLOWER

COLONETTE

89. Piscina, 14th century. All Saints, North Moreton, Berkshire

CROCKET

90. Easter sepulchre, 14th century. All Saints, Hawton, Nottinghamshire

CANOPY

TRUMEAU

91. Doorway to Chapter House, late 13th century. York Minster

TESTER

SPLAY

WINDER

92. Jacobean pulpit. St Mary, Moulton St Mary, Norfolk

RETABLE

LINENFOLD
PANELLING

ALTAR

93. Altar, 16th century. St Leonard, Farleigh Hungerford, Somerset

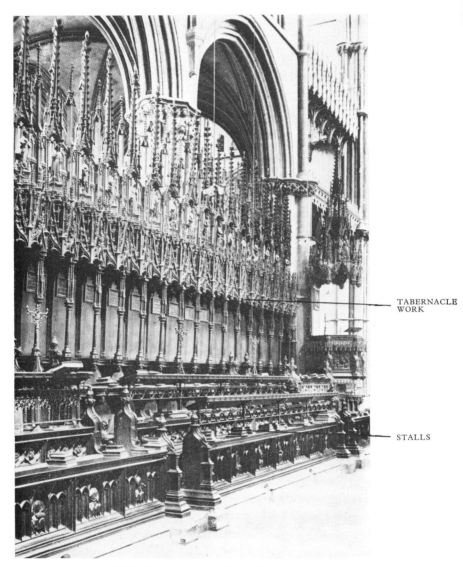

TABERNACLE
WORK

STALLS

94. Choir stalls, 14th century. Lincoln Cathedral

95. Poppyhead. 14th century. Winchester Cathedral, Hampshire

96. Misericord, 14th century. Lincoln Cathedral

97. Georgian box pews, St Andrew, Field Dalling, Norfolk

98. Sanctus bell-cote, 15th century. St Mary Magdalen, Newark, Nottinghamshire

99. Lych gate. All Saints, North Cerney, Gloucestershire

100. Encaustic tile, 13th century. Chapter House, Westminster Abbey

SPUR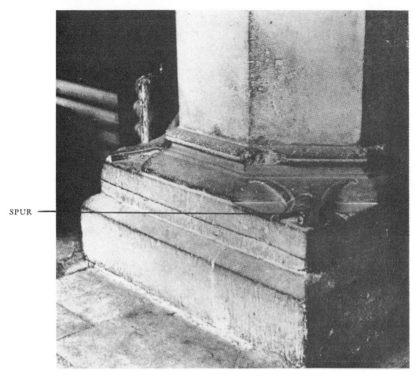

101. Late 12th century column and base. North choir arcade,
St Mary de Haura, New Shoreham, Sussex

PUTTO

102. Cartouche, 17th century. St Mary, Bampton, Oxfordshire

103. Columna Rostrata, Monument to Admiral John Baker, 1716. Westminster Abbey

104. Gadrooning to the monument to Lady Williamson, late 17th century. Holy Trinity, Loddon, Norfolk

BALDACHINO

105. Baldachino. Monument to the Countess of Derby, *c.* 1636.
St Mary, Harefield, Middlesex

CURTAIN
WALL
INNER
BAILEY
OUTER
BAILEY
BASTION

MOAT

BARBICAN

106. Beaumaris Castle, Anglesey. Late 13th and early 14th century

TURRET

MACHICOLA-
TION

TOWER

POSTERN

MOAT

107. Bodiam Castle, Sussex. Late 14th century

PORTCULLIS

108. Portcullis, Bodiam Castle, Sussex. Late 14th century

BARTIZAN

109. Drawbridge, Cawdor Castle, Nairn, Scotland. 1454 but restored

KEEP

110. Keep, 11th century. Rochester Castle, Kent

BATTLE-
MENT

ARROW
LOOP

PARAPET

RAMPART
WALK

SCARP

RAMPART

III. Caesar's Tower, late 14th century. Warwick Castle

GARDEROBE

SHELL KEEP

MOTTE

FOSSE

112. Shell keep, early 12th century. Restormel Castle, Cornwall

SPUR

113. South-west tower, c. 1300. Goodrich Castle, Herefordshire

BARTIZAN

CORBELLING

MACHICOLA-
TION

GARDEROBE

114. Chipchase Castle, Northumberland. Mid 14th century and Jacobean

115. Pele Tower, *c.* 1300. Corbridge, Northumberland

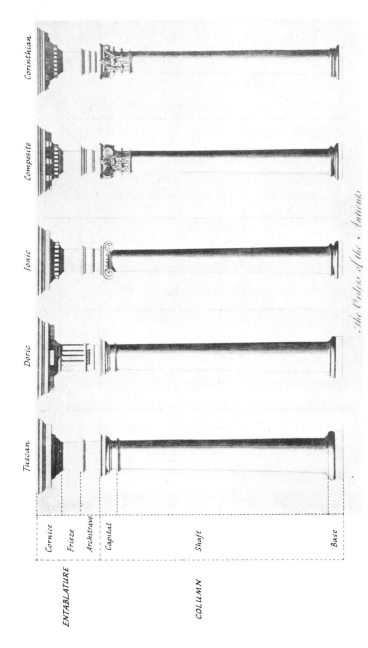

116. The Five Orders from Chambers's *Treatise on Civil Architecture*, 1759

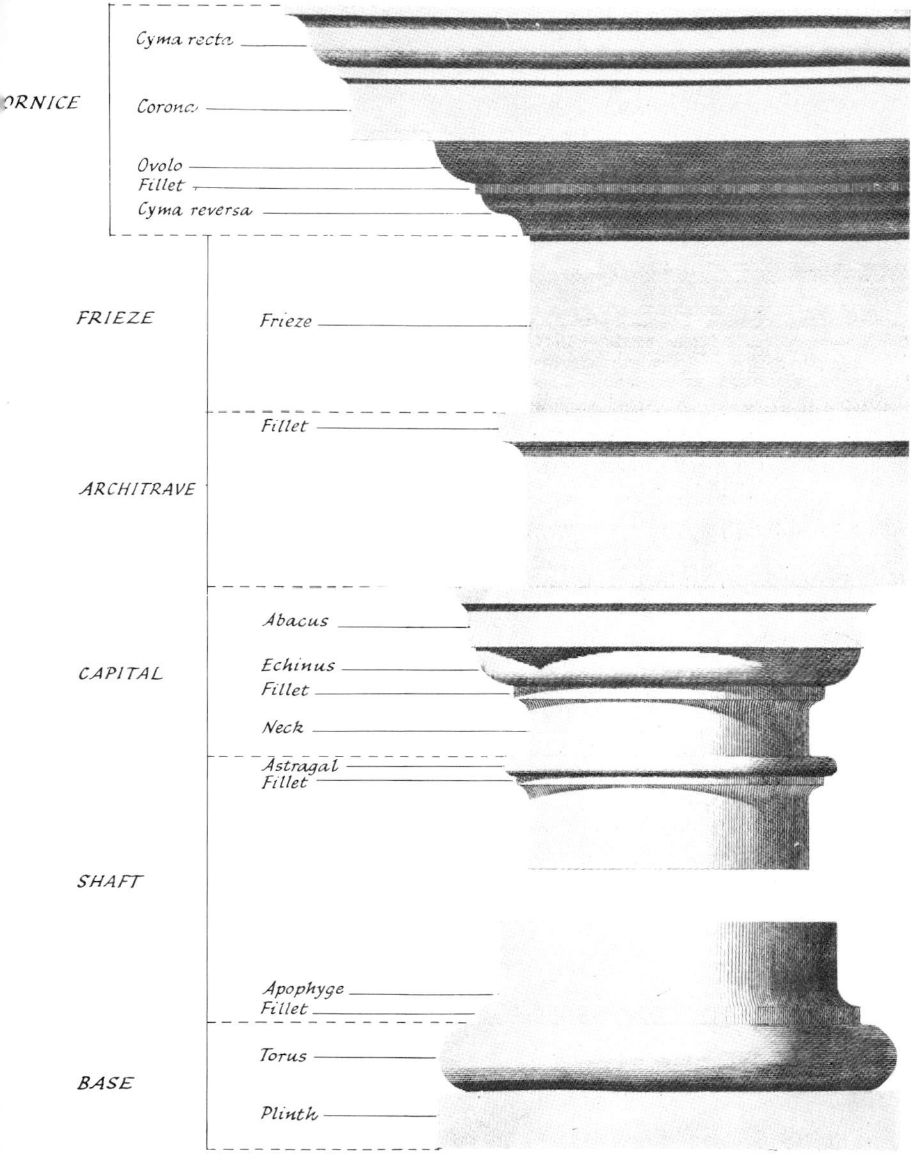

CORNICE
- Cyma recta
- Corona
- Ovolo
- Fillet
- Cyma reversa

FRIEZE
- Frieze

ARCHITRAVE
- Fillet

CAPITAL
- Abacus
- Echinus
- Fillet
- Neck
- Astragal
- Fillet

SHAFT

BASE
- Apophyge
- Fillet
- Torus
- Plinth

117. Tuscan order from Chambers's *Treatise on Civil Architecture*, 1759

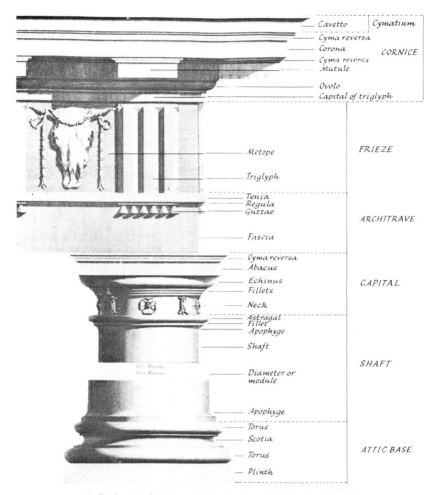

Cavetto | Cymatium
Cyma reversa
Corona
Cyma reversa | CORNICE
Mutule

Ovolo
Capital of triglyph

Metope | FRIEZE

Triglyph

Tenia
Regula
Guttae | ARCHITRAVE

Fascia

Cyma reversa
Abacus
Echinus | CAPITAL
Fillets

Neck

Astragal
Fillet
Apophyge

Shaft | SHAFT

Diameter or
module

Apophyge

Torus
Scotia
Torus | ATTIC BASE

Plinth

118. Doric order from Chambers's *Treatise on Civil Architecture*, 1759

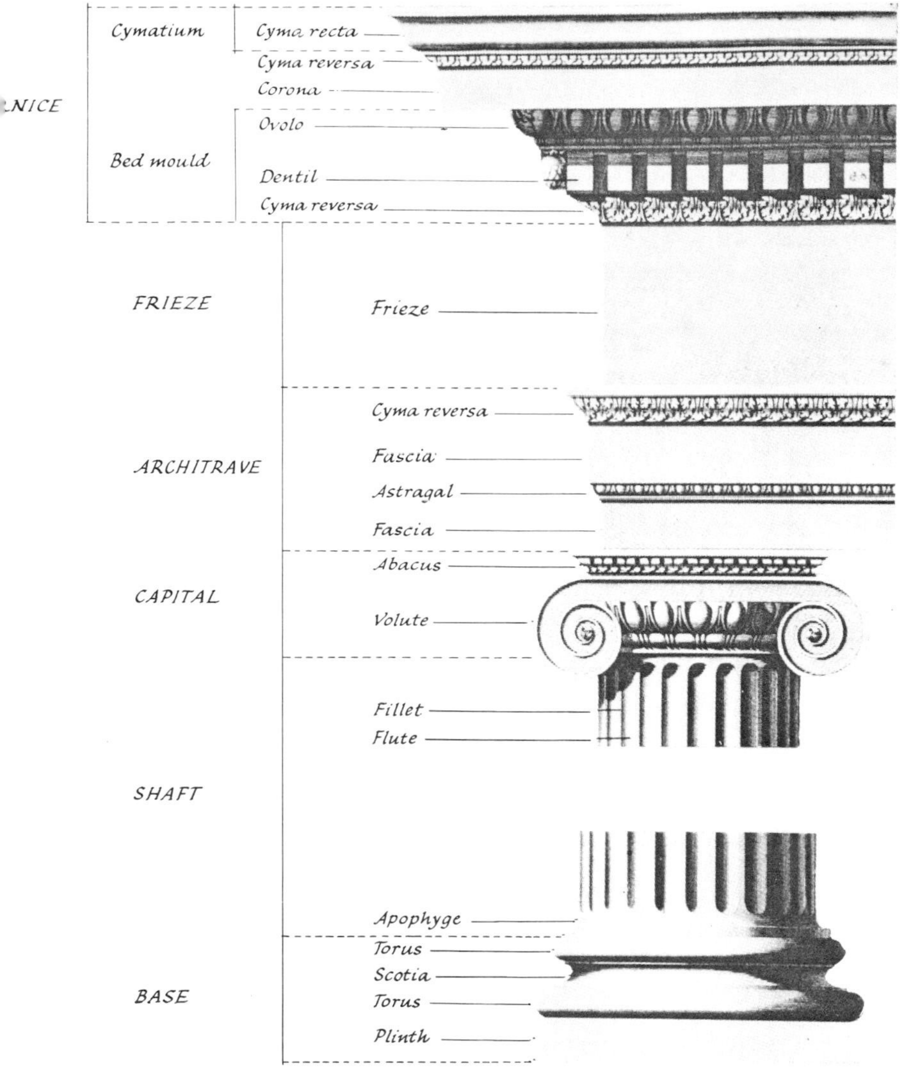

CORNICE

Cymatium
- Cyma recta
- Cyma reversa
- Corona

Bed mould
- Ovolo
- Dentil
- Cyma reversa

FRIEZE — Frieze

ARCHITRAVE
- Cyma reversa
- Fascia
- Astragal
- Fascia

CAPITAL
- Abacus
- Volute

- Fillet
- Flute

SHAFT

BASE
- Apophyge
- Torus
- Scotia
- Torus
- Plinth

119. Ionic order from Chambers's *Treatise on Civil Architecture*, 1759

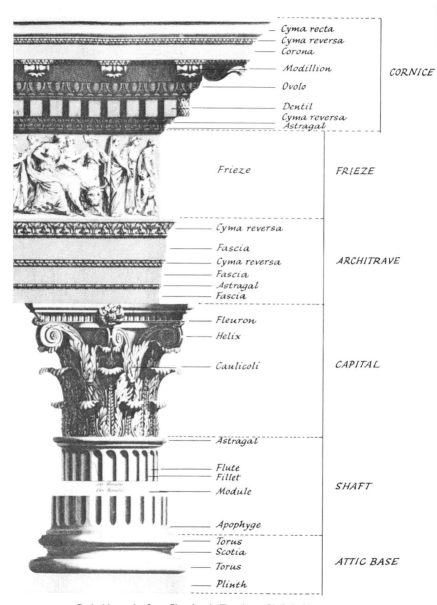

Cyma recta
Cyma reversa
Corona
Modillion
Ovolo
Dentil
Cyma reversa
Astragal

CORNICE

Frieze

FRIEZE

Cyma reversa
Fascia
Cyma reversa
Fascia
Astragal
Fascia

ARCHITRAVE

Fleuron
Helix
Caulicoli

CAPITAL

Astragal
Flute
Fillet
Module
Apophyge

SHAFT

Torus
Scotia
Torus
Plinth

ATTIC BASE

120. Corinthian order from Chambers's *Treatise on Civil Architecture*, 1759

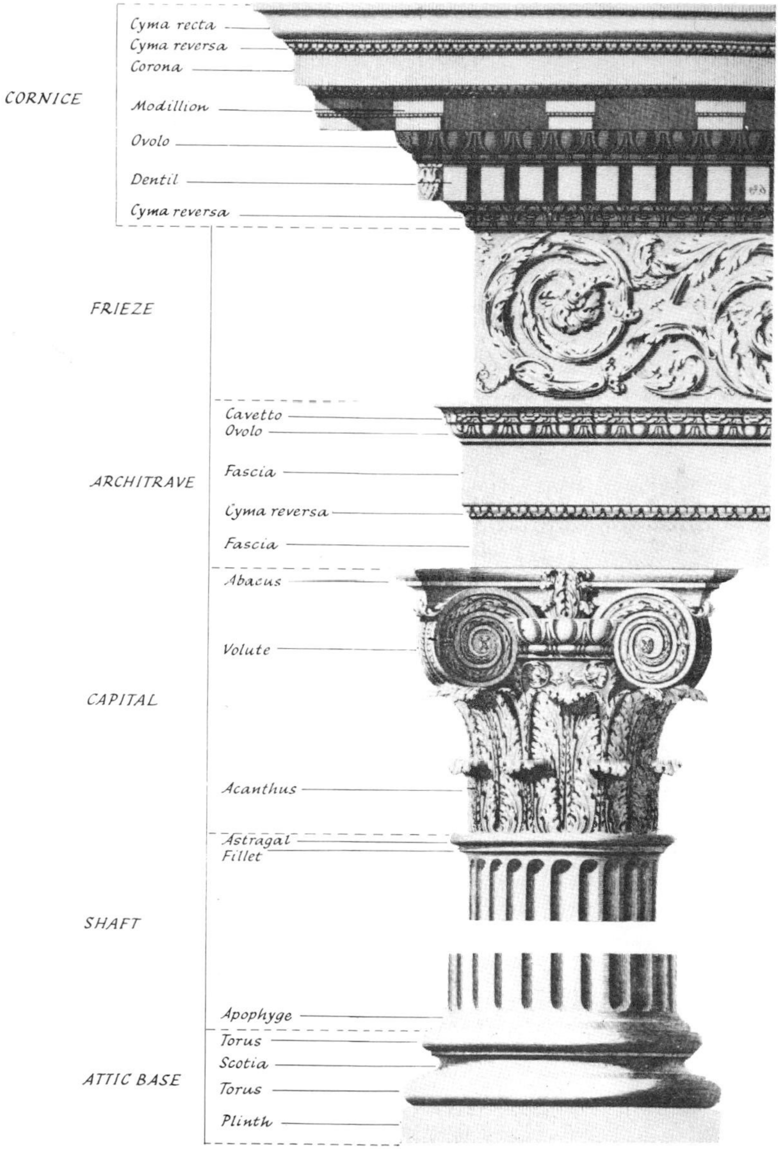

CORNICE
Cyma recta
Cyma reversa
Corona
Modillion
Ovolo
Dentil
Cyma reversa

FRIEZE

ARCHITRAVE
Cavetto
Ovolo
Fascia
Cyma reversa
Fascia

CAPITAL
Abacus
Volute
Acanthus
Astragal
Fillet

SHAFT

ATTIC BASE
Apophyge
Torus
Scotia
Torus
Plinth

121. Composite order from Chambers's *Treatise on Civil Architecture*, 1759

CYMA
REVERSA

CORONA

OVOLO

FRIEZE

SOFFIT
ARCHITRAVE
ABACUS

ECHINUS
NECK
ASTRAGAL

SHAFT

122. Colonnade. Queen Anne's Walk, Barnstaple, Devon. 1708

CYMA RECTA
CYMA REVERSA
CORONA
SOFFIT
MODILLION
DENTIL
FRIEZE
ARCHITRAVE
ABACUS
HELIX
CAULICOLI
ASTRAGAL
APOPHYGE
PATERA

123. Corinthian order. Portico, Kedleston Hall, Derbyshire. Robert Adam, 1760–70

LOUVER

124. Abbot's Kitchen, 14th century. Glastonbury Abbey, Somerset

CROW-STEP
GABLE

ORIEL
WINDOW

OVERSAILING
COURSE

125. Prior's House, 16th century. Castle Acre Priory, Norfolk

126. Freston Tower, Suffolk. Tudor

VALLEY

COURSED
RUBBLE

127. Dovecot, 13th century. Chipping Campden, Gloucestershire

128. Almshouses. Chipping Campden, Gloucestershire. 1612

SPIRELET

CASTELLATED

HOOD MOULD

129. Quadrangle, 15th century and after. All Souls College, Oxford

EXTRUDED
CORNER

130. Doddington Hall, Lincolnshire. Elizabethan, 1593. Perhaps by Robert Smithson

131. Jacobean south entrance. Hatfield House, Hertfordshire. 1611

RELIEVING
ARCH

132. St Catherine's Court, near Bath, Somerset. Early 17th century

SHAPED
GABLE

BAY
WINDOW

133. Gatehouse. Stanway, Gloucestershire. Early 17th century

LANTERN
PLATFORM
DORMER
ATTIC
EAVES

SASH

STRING
COURSE

PERRON

134. Coleshill House, Berkshire. Sir Roger Pratt, 1650–62

DUTCH
GABLE

BULL'S EYE
WINDOW

QUOIN

PAVILION

BASEMENT

135. Raynham Hall, Norfolk. The centre perhaps by Inigo Jones, c. 1625

PARAPET

ESCUTCHEON

NICHE

VENETIAN
WINDOW

VOUSSOIR

SKEWBACK

BANDED
COLUMN

VERMICULA-
TION

136. Screen with portal. Castle Ashby, Northamptonshire.
17th century, attributed to Inigo Jones

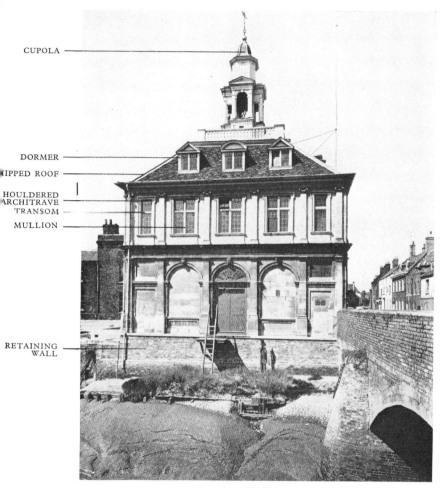

CUPOLA

DORMER

HIPPED ROOF

SHOULDERED
ARCHITRAVE

TRANSOM

MULLION

RETAINING
WALL

137. Carolean Customs House, Kings Lynn, Norfolk. Henry Bell, 1683

BLOCKING
COURSE

LUNETTE

BANDED
RUSTICATIO

138. Tower of Kitchen Court, Blenheim Palace, Oxfordshire.
Sir John Vanbrugh, Baroque *c.* 1707

LANTERN

DOME

DRUM

ACROTERION

139. St Paul's Cathedral, west front. Sir Christopher Wren, 1675–1710

BALUSTER
BALUSTRADE

PORTICO

STYLOBATE

140. Doric prostyle temple. Chatsworth, Derbyshire. William Talman, *c.* 1690

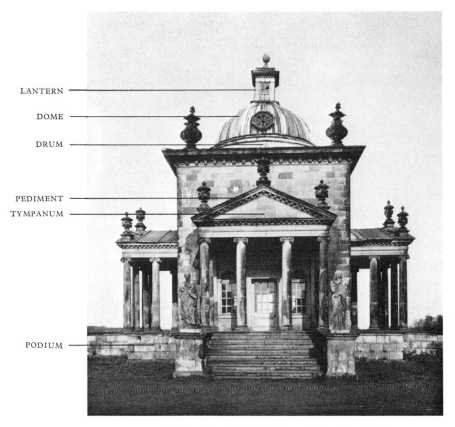

LANTERN

DOME

DRUM

PEDIMENT
TYMPANUM

PODIUM

141. Belvedere Temple with Doric tetrastyle porticoes. Castle
Howard, Yorkshire. Sir John Vanbrugh, 1725

142. Chicheley Hall, Buckinghamshire. Francis Smith, c. 1729

ATTIC
ORDER

APRON

GIANT
ORDER

PEDESTAL

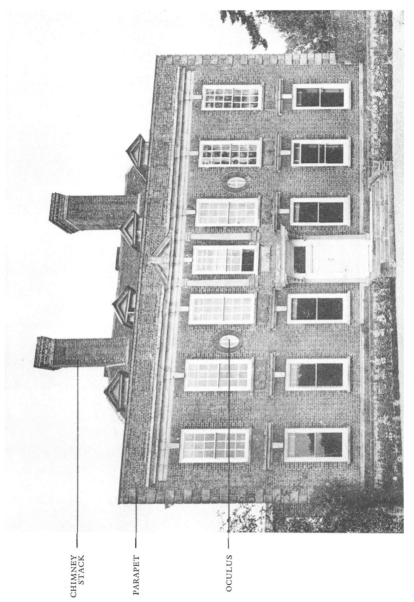

CHIMNEY STACK

PARAPET

OCULUS

143. Westwell House, Tenterden, Kent. Queen Anne style

OPEN
SEGMENTAL
PEDIMENT

PILASTER

144. Gazebo, Early Georgian. Alkerton Grange, Eastington, Gloucestershire

145. Obelisk and Rotunda, Chiswick House, Middlesex. Lord Burlington, *c.* 1725

DOME

DRUM

DIOCLETIAN
WINDOW

PIANO
NOBILE

TERM

146. Chiswick House, Middlesex. Lord Burlington and William Kent, c. 1725

COLONNADE

BALUSTRADE

VOUSSOIR

ABUTMENT

PIER

147. Palladian Bridge, Wilton House, Wiltshire. Roger Morris and the 9th Earl of Pembroke, 1736

ANTA

148. Portico in antis, Sudbrooke House, Surrey. James Gibbs, 1726–28

ACROTERION

EYE

ENGAGED COLUMN

149. Spencer House, London. John Vardy, 1756-65

MEZZANINE

150. Mezzanine. Somerset House, London. Sir William Chambers, 1776–80

CHAMFERED
RUSTICATION

151. The Orangery, Kew Gardens, Surrey. Sir William Chambers, 1761

152. Gothic Revival garden house, mid 18th century. Frampton, Gloucestershire

153. Castle style, Taymouth Castle, Perthshire. Early 19th century

154. Garden pavilion, Burleigh House, Northamptonshire. Capability Brown, *c.* 1767

155. Folly. Dallington, Sussex. Called the Sugar Loaf. Early 19th century

156. Thatched cottage Ornée, late 18th century lodge to Costessey Park, Norfolk

157. Grotto, perhaps by Josiah Lane, *c.* 1740. Pains Hill, Surrey

158. Ivy Lodge, Cirencester Park, Gloucestershire. Perhaps by the 1st Earl of Bathurst, c. 1735

OVERHANG

ARCADE

LOGGIA

159. Picturesque villa. Cronkhill, Shropshire. John Nash, c. 1802

BALCONY

RENDERING

160. Terrace, *c.* 1827. Alexander Square, London, S.W.7

VERANDA

161. Regency veranda. Richmond Terrace, Bristol, Somerset. Early 19th century

BATTER

162. Egyptian Revival mausoleum. Blickling Hall, Norfolk. Joseph Bonomi, 1793

ANTEFIX

CARYATID

VITRUVIAN
OPENING

STYLOBATE

163. Greek Revival. North porch, St Pancras Church, London. William Inwood, 1819

CRUCK

STUD

164. Vernacular Elizabethan cottage. Didbrook, Gloucestershire

HALF-HIPPED ROOF

OVERHANG

EAVES

PORCH

265. Tudor farm-house. Grantham Hill, Lamberhurst, Kent

GAMBRIEL ROOF

LEAN-TO ROOF

166. Newark Mill, Pyrford, Surrey. Early 19th century

MANSARD
ROOF

WEATHER
BOARDING

167. Early 19th-century houses, Lamberhurst, Kent

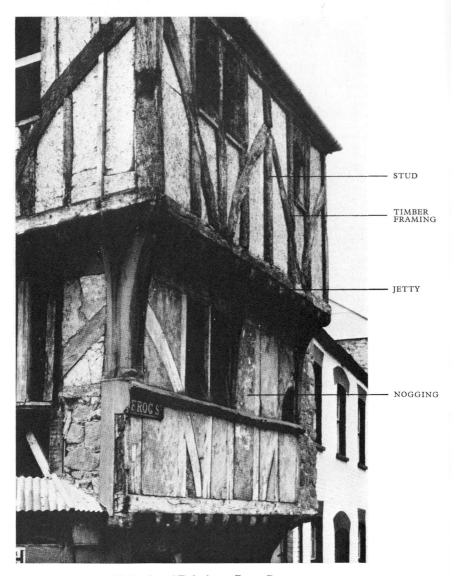

STUD

TIMBER
FRAMING

JETTY

NOGGING

168. Timber framed Tudor house, Exeter, Devon

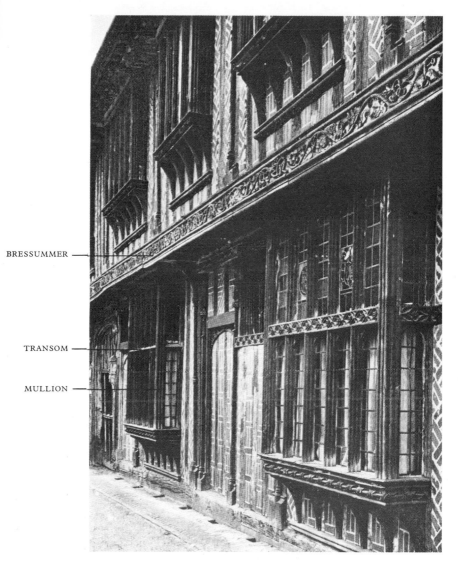

BRESSUMMER

TRANSOM

MULLION

169. Paycocke's House, Great Coggeshall, Essex. *c.* 1500

SHOULDERED ARCHITRAVE

170. Artisan mannerism. Doorway, St Helen, Bishopsgate, London. 1633

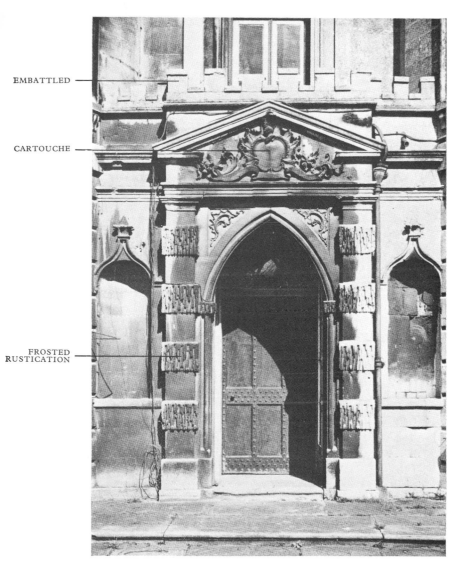

EMBATTLED

CARTOUCHE

FROSTED
RUSTICATION

171. Rococo Gothic. Arno's Court, Bristol. *c.* 1760, perhaps by James Bridges

BROKEN
PEDIMENT

BANDED
COLUMN

ROCK FACED
RUSTICATION

172. The Belvedere, Erith, Kent. Palladian wing by Isaac Ware, *c.* 1750

KEYSTONE

173. Doorway with Gibbs Surround. Melbourne Hall, Derbyshire. *c.* 1725

VENETIAN
DOOR

174. Venetian doorway. Claydon House, Buckinghamshire.
Sir Thomas Robinson, *c.* 1765

175. Palladian motif. The Triumphal Arch, Wilton House, Wiltshire. Sir William Chambers, 1759;
loggias by James Wyatt, c. 1800

TROPHY

176. Portal of the Citadel, Plymouth, Devon. 1670

PATERA

SWAG

FRET

VERMICU-
LATED
RUSTICATION

177. Gate piers. Chiswick House, Middlesex. Lord Burlington, *c.* 1728

COPING

BAS-RELIEF

RAMP

178. Bridge. St John's College, Cambridge. Robert Grumbold, 1709-12

DRIP ———

179. Rainwater head. The Mausoleum, Castle Howard, Yorkshire.
Nicholas Hawksmoor, 1729–36

JOIST

BEAM

EMBRASURE

180. Window embrasure, *c.* 12th century. Boothby Pagnell Manor House, Lincolnshire

FASCIA

FANLIGHT

BOW
WINDOW

181. Regency shop front. 34 Haymarket, London

PULVINATED
FRIEZE

BAY LEAF

BRACKET

SASH

REVEAL

BALUSTER

182. Window, Mereworth Castle, Kent. Colin Campbell, *c.* 1722

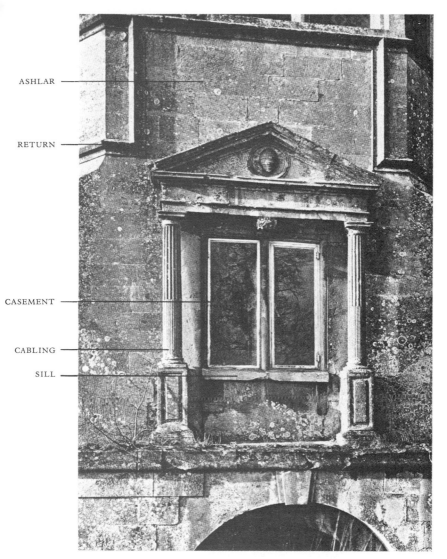

ASHLAR

RETURN

CASEMENT

CABLING

SILL

183. Elizabethan aedicule. Newark Park, Gloucestershire

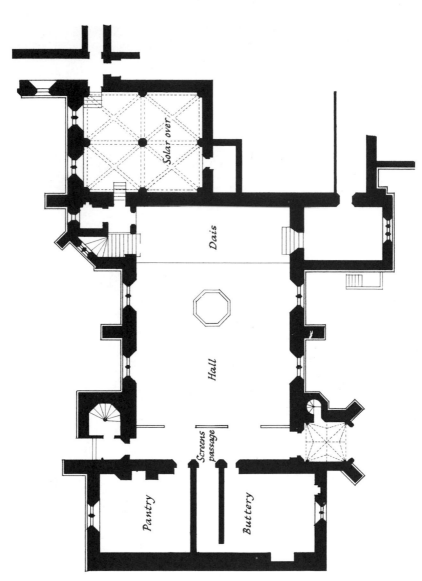

Solar over

Dais

Hall

Screens passage

Pantry

Buttery

184. Plan of Penshurst Place, Kent. 14th century and later

PENDANT

185. Long gallery, Blickling Hall, Norfolk. c. 1620

SPUR

186. Tudor Spur. Rufford Old Hall, Lancashire. *c.* 1480

STILE

WAINSCOT

REEDING

RAIL

MUNTIN

187. Elizabethan internal porch. Sherborne Castle, Dorset

MINSTREL
GALLERY

188. Hall and minstrels' gallery. Penshurst Place, Kent. 15th century

SPIRAL
COLUMN

189. Chimney piece, late 17th century. Tredegar Park, Monmouthshire

LATTICE

BUCRANIUM

STRAPWORK

GROTESQUE

190. Jacobean screen, Knole, Kent. Early 17th century

SCROLLED
PEDIMENT

SWAG

OPEN
PEDIMENT

FESTOON

FIREPLACE

191. Chimney piece. Double Cube Room, Wilton House, Wiltshire. John Webb, *c.* 1650

BOLECTION
MOULDING

BEAD

FIELDED
PANEL

FESTOON

CHIMNEY
PIECE

CHIMNEY
BREAST

192. Chimney piece. Chatsworth, Derbyshire. William Talman
and Samuel Watson, *c.* 1690

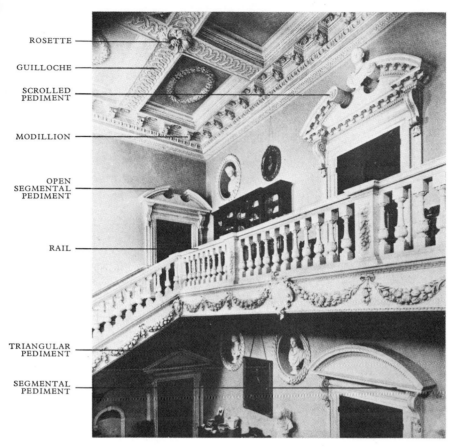

ROSETTE

GUILLOCHE

SCROLLED
PEDIMENT

MODILLION

OPEN
SEGMENTAL
PEDIMENT

RAIL

TRIANGULAR
PEDIMENT

SEGMENTAL
PEDIMENT

193. Staircase. Coleshill, Berkshire. Sir Roger Pratt, *c.* 1650

EXTRADOS

INTRADOS

PENDENTIVE

194. The Great Hall, Castle Howard, Yorkshire. Sir John Vanbrugh
and Nicholas Hawksmoor, *c.* 1700

COVE

COFFER

BUCRANIUM

ANGULAR
CAPITAL

VOLUTE

BAS-RELIEF

VITRUVIAN
SCROLL

EXEDRA

FRET

195. Egyptian Hall, Holkham, Norfolk. Lord Burlington and William Kent, *c.* 1735

BEAD

196. Overdoor. Drawing room, Beningbrough Hall, Yorkshire.
William Thornton, early 18th century

BEAD AND
REEL

CYMA RECTA

FILLET

EGG AND
DART
CAVETTO

MITRE

197. Overdoor. Chiswick House, Middlesex. William Kent, *c.* 1725

CHIMNEY
BREAST

ATLAS

PLINTH
BLOCK

198. Chimney piece. Rushbrooke Hall, Suffolk. c. 1740

MEDALLION

199. Chinoiserie. North Hall, Claydon House, Buckinghamshire. Plasterwork by Mr Lightfoot, *c.* 1765

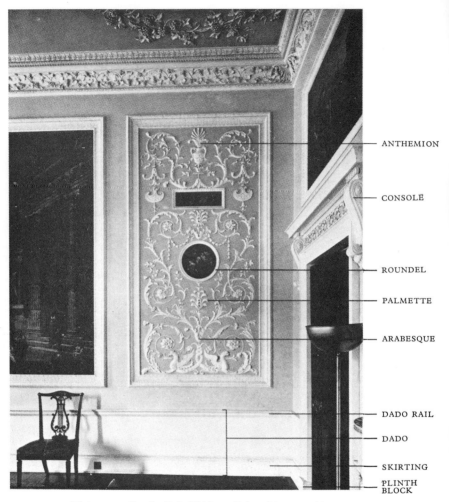

ANTHEMION

CONSOLE

ROUNDEL

PALMETTE

ARABESQUE

DADO RAIL

DADO

SKIRTING

PLINTH
BLOCK

200. Dining room, Osterley Park, Middlesex. Robert Adam, *c.* 1766

CORNICE

MANTEL-
SHELF

SURBASE

DIE

PLINTH

201. The Hall, Osterley Park, Middlesex. Robert Adam, *c.* 1766

202. Etruscan Room, Osterley Park, Middlesex. Robert Adam, 1775

DADO

203. Print Room, Woodhall Park, Hertfordshire. Thomas Leverton architect, c. 1780, the Prints laid out by R. Parker in 1782

204. Doglegged stair. Audley End House, Saffron Walden, Essex. *c.* 1610

205. Spiral stair. Dover Castle, Kent. 1180–86

WELL

206. Geometrical stair. Queen's House, Greenwich. Inigo Jones, *c.* 1635

207. Geometrical stair. Home House, Portman Square, London. Robert Adam, 1774–76

208. Open well stair. King Charles Block, Greenwich Hospital, London. John Webb, *c.* 1668

NEWEL —

TREAD —

WALL
STRING —

209. Staircase. St Martin-in-the-Fields, London. James Gibbs, 1722

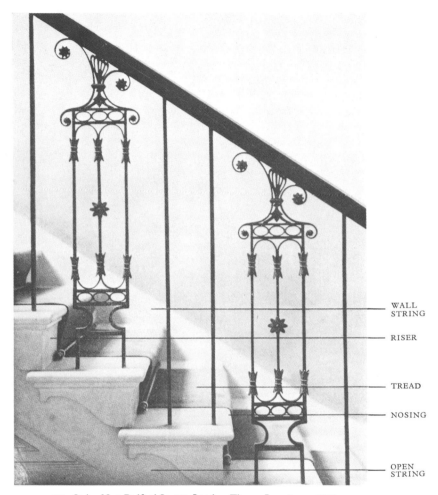

WALL
STRING

RISER

TREAD

NOSING

OPEN
STRING

210. Stairs. No 1 Bedford Square, London. Thomas Leverton, *c.* 1775

RAMP

WALL
STRING

OPEN
STRING

NOSING

TREAD

RISER

CURTAIL
STEP

211. Staircase. Claydon House, Buckinghamshire. *c.* 1770

POINTING

212i. English bond brickwork

212ii. Flemish bond brickwork

212iii. Norman herringbone work. St Peter, Southrop, Gloucestershire

212iv. Heading bond brickwork

213. Gauged brickwork. The Dutch House, Kew Gardens, Surrey. 1631

OVERHANG

POINTING

LINTEL

214. Random rubble, Penryn, Cornwall

CANTILEVER

215. Wattle and daub. Bignor, Sussex

216. Flushwork, 15th century. St Mary, Woolpit, Suffolk

THATCH

COB

217. Dunsford village, Devonshire

CREST TILE

BARGE BOAR[D]

PARGETTIN[G]

LATTICE

218. The Ancient House, Clare, Suffolk. 1473

SILL

KEYSTONE

FANLIGHT

VERMICU-
LATED
COADE
STONE

JAMB

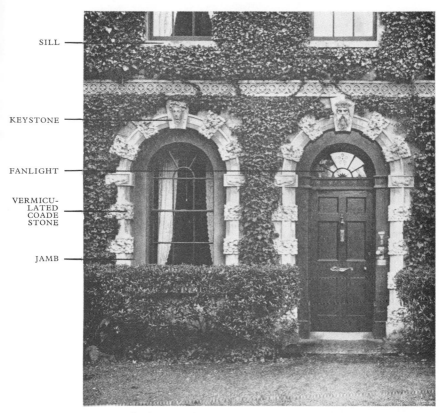

219. Coade stone embellishments to Belmont, Lyme Regis, Dorset. *c.* 1785

220. Tile hanging. High Street, Burwash, Sussex

221. Slate hanging. The Nunnery, Dunster, Somerset. 14th or 15th century

222. Crinkle crankle wall. Henham, Suffolk. 18th century

223. Barn on staddle stones. Cowdray Park, Sussex

224. Spur stone. Clink Street, London, S.E.1.